Love,

Momma D

Helping Parents Get to the Heart of Parenting From the Heart

Darla Noble

eLectio Publishing

Little Elm, TX

www.eLectioPublishing.com

Love, Momma D: Helping Parents Get to the Heart of Parenting From the Heart
By Darla Noble

ISBN-13: 978-1-63213-328-1
Published by eLectio Publishing, LLC
Little Elm, Texas
http://www.eLectioPublishing.com

Printed in the United States of America

5 4 3 2 1 eLP 20 19 18 17 16

The eLectio Publishing editing team is comprised of: Christine LePorte, Lori Draft, Sheldon James, Court Dudek, and Kaitlyn Campbell.

Publisher's Note
The publisher does not have any control over and does not assume any responsibility for author or third-party websites or their content.

CONTENTS

Introduction

In the daily experiences of diapering, homework, extracurricular activities, curfews, and everything else that goes along with raising kids, parents often forget the absolute most valuable "thing" every parent needs and the one that every child deserves…**unconditional love.**

Unconditional love is that "just because" kind of love. It is a love that doesn't have to be earned or is given because of the way a child looks or what they are capable of. Unconditional love is given for no other reason than your child lives and breathes.

Unconditional love encourages, disciplines, puts boundaries in place, allows children the freedom to learn on their own, forgives, extends mercy, respects, appreciates, and is consistent.

Unconditional love is the kind of love God gives to us, his children and the kind of love he wants us to share back with our kids.

Momma D (that's me) knows what a blessing it is to experience unconditional love and to feel the sense of self-worth, security, and peace that comes from being loved this way. It's a feeling no child should be without. That's why I am committed to reminding and teaching parents and grandparents the hows and whys of unconditional love. Nothing I say is based on scientific formulas or is the result of research studies. The wisdom I share with you is based on actual life—my life as a mom and nanna. The lessons and reminders come from my heart in the hope they will go straight to yours so that you can pass them on to the special little ones (and not-so-little ones) in your life.

Love,
Momma D

Training Wheels Not Necessary

Our son, Zach, was three the first time he became a big brother. When John told him he had a baby sister, he was excited, but in the next minute, he said he thought all big brothers needed a bicycle instead of a tricycle.

How could anyone argue with reasoning like that? We couldn't. That's why the day after we brought Elizabeth home, John went to town and came home with a little blue bicycle for Zach. He was elated...except for one thing...that bike had training wheels, and (in Zach's words) big brothers didn't use training wheels. So...off came the training wheels. We figured Zach would either be able to ride without them or would soon figure out he needed them. John and I were sure the training wheels would be going back on, but we couldn't have been more wrong. In less than an hour, three-year-old Zach was riding that little blue bike around the yard like he'd been doing it for years.

I'm so glad we gave Zach the opportunity to try. If we would have refused him, telling him he wasn't ready to ride without the training wheels or that he couldn't do it, we would have been stifling his self-confidence and his ability to do what he knew in his heart he could do.

What about you? Do you hold your children back from trying new things? Do you deny them opportunities to grow their confidence and self-esteem because *you* don't think they're ready or capable? So what if they don't succeed? At least they will have tried. At least they won't have to wonder *what if*. At least they'll know you believe in them and want them to believe in themselves. Besides, most of the time you'll find that your children won't ask for these opportunities unless they really want them. And if they want something bad enough, they are going to give it all they've got—and that's what really matters most.

Zach wasn't a three-year-old with super powers that September day in 1986. He was a little boy who really wanted to ride a two-wheel bike because in his mind, that was what big brothers were supposed to be able to do...and so he did. I'd also like to think that being allowed to try rather than being told no has something to do with the fact that, over the years, he's proven himself to be highly proficient in operating anything on wheels.

Remember...your job as a parent is to love unconditionally, to foster your child's sense of self-worth and confidence, and to allow them opportunities to find out just who they really are.

Love,
Momma D

...for the Lord will be at your side and
will keep your foot from being snared.
~Proverbs 3:26 (NIV)

Move Over, Barbie—Betty Spaghetti Is on the Scene

Betty Spaghetti was a bendable doll made of rubber and plastic popular with little girls a few years ago. She was perky and colorful, and her feet, hands, and shoes were removable so they could be replaced with some that were even perkier and more colorful.

Her hair, legs, and arms were rubbery and twistable (ergo the name Betty Spaghetti) and could be shaped into a plethora of positions.

Take that, Barbie! I'd like to see you twist *your* unrealistically perfect legs into a figure eight! And I bet you can't make the letter *S* with your arms like Betty Spaghetti. Oh, and Betty's hair never looked like she just went through a wind tunnel.

At this point, you may be wondering why I'm singing the praises of Betty Spaghetti and making a good case against myself for being a Barbie-basher. Well, wonder no more…

As parents, we need to encourage our children to be more like Betty. We need to let them bend and twist to become who *they* are (that whole move to the beat of their own drum philosophy). We need to be careful not to push them or allow them to put on the rigid, hard exterior of what society views as the perfect (Barbie-like) child or teen.

In letting our children bend and twist into their own personality, we give them the gift of being happy and confident in who they are. If, however, we push or allow conformity to the world's unrealistic expectations, they'll end up feeling inadequate and convinced they will never measure up or be good enough. They'll snap like a piece of hard, uncooked spaghetti at the first sign of stress.

Just like spaghetti (the kind we eat) has to be immersed in hot water before it can be softened into what it is supposed to be, as parents, we need to bathe our children in the warmth of love, security, and grace to bend, twist, and navigate through life being the wonderful, unique individuals they are.

Love,
Momma D

But the Lord said to Samuel, "Do not consider his appearance or his height, for I have rejected him. The Lord does not look at the things people look at. People look at the outward appearance, but the Lord looks at the heart."
~1ˢᵗ Samuel 16:7 (NIV)

Momma, You So Pwetty

Zach was always a happy and healthy little guy. His big brown eyes sparkled, and his sweet smile never failed to make my day. But one day when Zach was a little over a year old, he woke up with a fever and an earache. When I leaned down over him in his bed to kiss him and take his temperature, he looked up at me and said, "Momma, you so pwetty."

My heart instantly melted. My little boy thought I was 'pwetty' on the outside. But did he see me as 'pwetty' on the inside, too?

What do your children see when they look at you? Do they see a mom or dad who gives love freely and without conditions? Do they see a mom or dad who treats their other parent with respect…if not love *and* respect? Do they see a mom or dad who has integrity and honor? Do they see a mom or dad who loves them for who they are…period? Do they see a mom or dad who lives their faith and is the same person no matter where they are or who they're with? Do they see a mom or dad who demonstrates a strong work ethic? Do they see a mom or dad who values family and home over money and status? Do they see a mom or dad who will always be there for them… no matter what?

I'm sure there have been times in Zach's life (and the lives of my other children) when they haven't always thought I was so 'pwetty,' but there has never been a time in their lives when they haven't known they have my unconditional and undying love.

I hope and pray you can say the same.

Love,
Momma D

Her children arise and call her blessed; her husband also, and
he praises her.
~Proverbs 31:28 (NIV)

A Garbage Disposal Is No Place for a Pet Fish...
Or Your Kids

That moment when you have to stick your hand down the drain or garbage disposal because you drop your fish down there while cleaning its bowl...yah, I just had that moment. I sure hope Merida the fish is as brave as its namesake Disney Princess.

This was what I posted on my Facebook page a while back. That's right—Momma D somehow let Merida the fish land in the garbage disposal instead of back into the bowl after changing the water. Needless to say, I was horrified! I also immediately shoved my hand down into the garbage disposal where Merida was thrashing around. Grabbing the fish with two fingers (so I wouldn't squish it), I pulled it out and quickly dropped my little fish back into its bowl...where I just knew I would find it floating on top of the water by the end of the day.

But wait! That's not what happened. Merida continued to swim around in the bowl as if nothing happened. Merida the fish had been to the garbage disposal and back *and* lived to "tell" about it.

Some of the comments I received following my post on Facebook implied (not so subtly, I might add) that I should have just flipped the switch and been done—that I'd missed my chance. I know these things were said in jest, and I was not offended in the least, but I couldn't have disagreed more. What can I say—I like Merida.

Merida's rescue also reminded me of something very important when it comes to parenting our children: NEVER GIVE UP and NEVER LET ANYONE MAKE YOUR CHILD FEEL LIKE HE/SHE IS DISPOSABLE.

All too often, children with physical or emotional disabilities are pushed aside to make way for the "smart kids" or kids who have potential (as if any child doesn't have potential!). Children who rebel, trap themselves in addictions, or who fall into the depths of low self-esteem and self-destruction are often labeled outcasts, lost causes, or detriments to society.

Don't let this happen to your child. Don't do this to your child. Every child struggles now and again—some more than others. The severity of their struggles isn't the point. What *is* the point is that they know you are there for them—ready to grab hold of them if they need help getting out of life's garbage disposals and to encourage them to be the incredible, unique, and beautiful person they are.

Love,

Momma D

For you created my inmost being; you knit me together in my mother's womb. I praise you because I am fearfully and wonderfully made; your works are wonderful, I know that full well
~Psalm 139:13-14 (NIV)

Who Needs a Disney Princess When I Have You?

The other day, my daughter Olivia called to share a special mom-moment with me. Reuben woke up singing "The Itsy, Bitsy Spider," and she just stood outside his bedroom door listening with joy in her heart and being thankful she was able to enjoy and experience these moments in her son's life.

Within the last two weeks, I've also:

- Skyped with my daughter, Emma, to share her excitement over Essie pulling up to stand on her own two feet…by herself.
- Shared my oldest daughter Elizabeth's concern for Laney's rash and her awe in the fact that this little girl can hold her pet rabbit in her arms and swing with him in her swing (and yes, Boots is a real rabbit).
- Been able to spend time with my daughter-in-law, Becca, laughing over the antics of Mack and Macy and watching her be the loving and patient yet firm mom that she is.

None of the events the girls shared with me are going to change the world, make the headlines, or make the kids (and their parents) rich and famous. But that's okay, because while The Little Mermaid and Belle have taken a back seat to Anna and Elsa, I know without a doubt that Reuben, Essie, Laney, Mackenzie, and Macy will never be pushed aside for someone with more sparkles, different songs, or a snowman that doesn't melt.

As parents, my girls understand it's the little things that make their children unique, precious, and irreplaceable. They understand that being a mom is about taking the time to notice and enjoy the little things, tucking them away in their hearts for someday when (all too quickly) the kids are grown and they (my girls) are where I'm at now.

How about you? Are you taking the time to really enjoy your children? Are you giving them the time and opportunity to experience life the way a kid should?

Don't be too busy to miss out on the simple yet special things that happen in your child's life—the things that steal your heart and make it sing like a Disney Princess.

Love,
Momma D

May your father and mother rejoice; may she who gave you birth be joyful!
~Proverbs 23:25 (NIV)

Go Ahead...Write Your Own "Mom Song"

Have you heard the "Mom Song" by Anita Renfroe? Sung (I use that word loosely) to the tune of the "William Tell Overture," she condenses what she believes to be a mom's twenty-four-hour discourse with her children into a song lasting just under three minutes.

Anyway...I heard the song on the radio the other morning, and as I listened, two things came to mind:

- The words *I love you* were wedged into the song (near the end) and only once.
- The words *I'm sorry* were not mentioned at all.

Okay, so I know the song is meant to be satirical. I also know there's a bit of truth in it, too. I'm not too proud to admit I've played the because-I-said-so card a few times. So in some ways, the song is good for a chuckle or two. But what I don't want is for parents to listen to this song and nod their heads in agreement, thinking this is what parenting is all about.

Don't forget that for every "brush your teeth," "don't make me tell you twice," and "no dessert if you don't eat your dinner," there need to be at least a dozen "I love yous."

Don't forget that two of the most powerful words you will ever say to your child are *I'm sorry*. Saying I'm sorry is essential because, let's face it, you aren't always right. You do make mistakes, and your attitude isn't always what it should be. You're human—every parent is. In fact, parents are just as human as their children.

My intention is *not* to bash Anita Renfroe and her song, but at the same time, I want parents to remember that her rendition of the average day in the life of a mom is not what you should be striving for *or* willing to settle for. Your kids deserve more than that from you.

So go ahead…make up your own mom song—one that lets everyone know you view parenting as a privilege instead of a chore of never-ending reminders and police actions.

"I love you, Zach, Elizabeth, Olivia, and Emma Dale and I'm sorry for (you can fill in the blank)," sung to the tune of…

Love,
Momma D

A cheerful heart is good medicine, but a crushed spirit dries up the bones.
~Proverbs 17:22 (NIV)

All That and a Bag of Chips

One of the highlights of my kids' years when they were young was the Wyman Carnival—aka, the yearly fundraiser at the elementary school they attended. The Wyman Carnival was a typical school carnival—fish pond, cake walk, ring toss, popcorn, cotton candy, face painting, and everything else you would expect to find at an event such as this…including the cheap little prizes— ahem, I mean *treasures*—the kids collected for playing the games (over and over and over again).

Oh, who am I trying to kid—the carnival was fun for the parents, too. It was fun to supervise the games and watch the kids react to being at school but not *in* school and giddy with the excitement that came from the sense of freedom they had.

Yes, you heard me—most of us allowed our children to go from room to room to room with their siblings and friends without us tagging along behind them or telling them where to go and what to do. That's right—they were on their own. They decided how to spend their carnival tickets. They decided how to conduct themselves. They decided which prize to choose after playing a game. It was up to them to find their way from one room to another and to listen to and understand the rules of the game.

Do you see where I'm going with this? As a parent, you have to give your children the freedom to experience life on their own. You have to give your children a certain amount of freedom to make their own choices and decisions without looking over their shoulder to see if you approve or to acquiesce to what you think. You also have to give them these freedoms away from the confines of home. Giving them a choice between wearing a red shirt or a brown one or whether they want waffles or cereal for breakfast is a great place to start, but you have to let them use these same skills in public and with their peers.

Remember, if you give them the opportunity to do this at an early age while you are still able to influence and mold them, they will be better equipped to make good choices in a few years when you aren't nearly as cool in their eyes.

Our days as Wyman kids are long gone, but my kids will still tell you their favorite thing about the Wyman Carnival was feeling like they were all that and a bag of chips walking around without me. (Little did they know their freedom was actually a life lesson in self-discipline and responsibility).

I know it's not easy for parents to feel like this is an option these days—what with all the scary things happening out there. But there were scary things happening then, too. I just chose to educate and equip my kids to know how to respond and conduct themselves instead of leaving them to figure it out on their own when hovering over them was no longer an option. I hope you will do the same.

Love,
Momma D

I will instruct you and teach you in the way you should go; I
will counsel you with my loving eye on you.
~Psalm 32:8 (NIV)

Where Did I Come From?

My granny was born 1916. She was born into a large family who lived in a tiny house in the middle of the Ozarks. They were a farm family, and like so many others, worked hard for what they had. The results of all that hard work resulted in food for their table, clean clothes to wear, a strong work ethic, a lot of love for one another, and enough stories to fill a few books.

Oh, the stories Granny could tell—stories about snake bites, runaway wagons, community gatherings in their one-room school house, losing all their money when the banks fell 1929, putting a fire out on the roof...when she was several months pregnant, and on and on she could go. Those stories are forever ingrained in my mind, as well as in the minds of my children. And why shouldn't they be? They're great stories. But even more than that, these stories are our history. They tell us who we came from—the character, integrity, strength, and faith of the people responsible for our existence.

Today's society is *obsessed* with the newest and latest, the fastest and fanciest, and the best of the best. Even our education system is kicking history and grammar to the curb in an effort to try to mold an entire generation of students into scientists and engineers who can come up with the next best everything. As parents, you need to make sure you don't allow this to happen to your children.

Give them their history. Teach your children who and where they came from. Share your family's traditions and culture with them and teach them to embrace it and take ownership of it. Encourage and foster relationships between your children and their grandparents, aunts and uncles, and even great aunts and uncles and cousins. But that's not all...

Everyone loves a good story—especially one with which they can associate. So gather stories from family members and share them with your children for the purpose of making names and faces in photographs come to life.

People are always saying the only direction to go is forward and into the future. Now, while there is value and truth in that statement, it is equally important to remember that without a past there is no future, and without understanding the past, we cannot truly appreciate the future.

So, parents, I leave you with this: a plant needs both roots and leaves to survive. Your family's history serves as your child's roots, and the state of the plant's leaves represents how well a child allows that history to shape and influence their lives.

Love,

Momma D

Your statutes are my heritage forever; they are the joy of my heart.
~Psalm 119:111 (NIV)

A Bird in the Tree and Pretty Kitchen Curtains

In our family, we always took turns praying at the dinner table. On this particular evening, it was Emma's turn. She was three at the time, and it just so happened that her place at the table was directly across from the window over the kitchen sink.

The windows were open, and from where Emma was sitting, she could see the giant walnut tree in the backyard. So that evening as she started praying, Emma took particular delight in thanking God for just about everything—and I do mean everything…

"Thank you, Jesus, for today and for my family. Thank you for the pretty kitchen curtains and for the bird sitting in the tree outside, the cups on the table, and thank you for…"

At that point, Olivia interrupted to inform us that Emma didn't have her eyes closed—that she wouldn't be able to see a bird outside if she did.

Emma defensively said she really was thankful for the curtains and the bird and all the other things she'd been praying about. And that, I said, was a very good thing.

The next thing I did was to remind the rest of our children that praying is about a lot more than just closing your eyes and saying the right thing. I wanted them to learn a few things from their baby sister. I wanted them to embrace the familiarity and openness Emma felt when she prayed. I wanted them to see prayer as a way to talk *with* God rather than something they recite *to* God.

Over the years, we prayed many prayers of thanks for baby lambs and good grades. We prayed for lost and dying pets, horrible school bus drivers, cross country meets, less-than-stellar school teachers, and even good weather for trick-or-treating. We've given thanks. We've prayed for healing of family and friends. We've asked for guidance and direction. Some of these prayers were prayed with eyes open and some with eyes squeezed tightly shut. And you know what? God heard and answered every single prayer with all the love and concern that makes him God.

The lesson in all of this? To allow and encourage your children to make their relationship with God personal, genuine, and one in which they know that everything that matters to them matters to Him—kitchen curtains and birds sitting in a tree included.

Love,
Momma D

Do not be anxious about anything, but in every situation, by prayer and petition, with thanksgiving, present your requests to God. And the peace of God, which transcends all understanding, will guard your hearts and your minds in Christ Jesus.
~Philippians 4:6-7 (NIV)

Oopsie Daisy

My children typically played well together. But kids being kids, there were times when they…did not. There was even a time or two when these battles resulted in a casualty or two, Oopsie Daisy being one of them…

Elizabeth and Olivia were five and three years old when, for a reason I don't even remember, they began to argue. Olivia decided she would be the one to come out on top. So what did she do? She went in for the kill by grabbing up Elizabeth's Oopsie Daisy doll and breaking her little leg right off her little plastic body.

Olivia's victory was short-lived, however, as justice was served swiftly and appropriately. While this did little to mend Elizabeth's broken heart or Oopsie's leg, I learned a very important lesson that day—well, actually two very important lessons.

Lesson one: It's impossible to fix a broken leg on an Oopsie Daisy doll even when Daddy tries.

Lesson two: You should never make your child say the words *I'm sorry*.

Making a child say they are sorry is making them tell a lie. That's right—if you make a child say something they do not mean, then they are lying. Instead, you need to concentrate your efforts on helping your child feel the *need* to ask for forgiveness and say they are sorry in *their* heart and mind…not yours.

Instead of making them say they're sorry, require them to listen while the person they hurt expresses their feelings or explains to them how their actions hurt them. Give them an opportunity to think about how they would feel if someone had done the same to them.

Either way, the desired end result is for your child to feel remorse and regret, both of which lead to *wanting* to apologize— and meaning it when they do.

FYI: These two ended up living together for a while when they left home and wouldn't hurt each other for anything...now. :)

Love,
Momma D

Be kind and compassionate to one another, forgiving each other, just as in Christ God forgave you.
~Ephesians 4:32 (NIV)

Parenting: A Life Sentence Worth Serving

As parents, we sometimes find ourselves dreaming of the day when our toddlers won't be tugging on our clothes and when we don't have to spend so much time shuttling kids from one soccer game to another and sleeping with one eye open waiting for them to come home on Friday and Saturday nights. But then that day comes…the day you drive out of the college dorm parking lot or are just one of many blowing kisses and bubbles as they drive away to begin their married life. And as you do, you are thinking…

- Where did the time go?
- It seems like only yesterday that I was…
- I wish those days hadn't gone by quite so fast.
- Life sure will be different now…now that they don't need me anymore.

Take it from Momma D—the years go by all too quickly. And it really does seem like only yesterday (or maybe last year) that I was the one making sure the tooth fairy did her job, feeling triumphant over a toddler's ninety-three trips to the potty, getting excited over new teeth, and sending out party invitations that said "I'm turning 1…or 2…or 4…or 7." What *isn't* true, however, is that once your children are grown, they don't need you anymore. You are their mother…their father. They will *always* need you. Don't believe me? Within the last couple of weeks, I've heard or read…

- Thanks, Mom, I really needed to hear that.
- I know I've already called you a bunch today, but…
- She was so brave…she let me pull that tooth right out.
- Mom, it's so hard when they're sick…it makes me feel so sad.
- I am so excited for Friday…I really need a mom-daughter day.
- Where's Dad? I want to talk to him, too.

- Dad and I had a great time the other day.
- Do you think Dad would mind…?

See? I told you…your kids will always need you. When it comes to being a mom or a dad, you are signing on for life. And you know what? I wouldn't have it any other way.

Love,

Momma D

Discipline your children, and they will give you peace; they will bring you the delights you desire.
~Proverbs 29:17 (NIV)

Psych!

Emma and I were in the yogurt shop one day enjoying our yogurt and going over her wedding plans. We were seated directly across from the yogurt bar, so we could not help but see and overhear what happened next…

A mom came in with her two small children—a boy and girl who looked to be between about five and seven years old. They stopped in front of the bowls where she said, "See, you take a bowl and then go over here and put the flavor of yogurt you want in the bowl." They moved down the line to stand in front of the yogurt dispensers, and she then guided them further down the line to stand in front of the toppings bar. The toppings bar (in case you don't know) is filled with containers of crushed candy bars, nuts, fruit, sprinkles, gummy bears, and all sorts of other goodies you can top your yogurt with. You could see the children's eyes getting bigger and bigger as they listened to their mom telling them that a person could choose as many of the goodies as they wanted to put on their yogurt. "And then," she said, "you take it to the person at the counter, pay for it, and then sit down to eat it."

Emma and I expected to see the children and their mother go back to the bowls and begin their delicious yogurt experience. But that is *not* what happened. Instead, the mother of these children said, "See, doesn't that look good? We aren't going to get any today, but we will come back soon, and when we do, you will know what to do. Okay?" And with that, the three of them walked back out the door—the children not saying a word.

BAM! Talk about taking the wind out of somebody's sails! Emma and I just looked at each other, not knowing whether to laugh or cry. Did she really just do that to her kids? Okay, I admit—we laughed. It was the I-can't-believe-that-just-happened kind of laugh. But we were not nearly as amused as we were dumbfounded and even sad for those two kids. Their little faces fell when their mom announced they were leaving empty-handed.

As parents, we need to be careful to not dangle the proverbial carrot in front of our children's faces—exasperating them. You cannot dangle your attention, support, time, encouragement, or even your love in front of them and then yank it away because you are too busy or because your children disappoint you or don't live up to your expectations. To do so sets them up for low self-esteem and insecurity, resentfulness, and rebellion that can lead to them making poor choices, and those may also be life-altering choices.

Our children aren't cups of yogurt, hoping you'll load them up with toppings of acceptance, trust, encouragement, and unconditional love. They are children—your children—and should never be made to feel as if they have to wait for some other day for you to parent from the heart.

Love,
Momma D

If I speak in the tongues of men or of angels, but do not have love, I am only a resounding gong or a clanging cymbal.
~1st Corinthians 13:1 (NIV)

When I Grow Up, I Want to Be a Teenager

"When I grow up, I want to be a teenager," Olivia said whenever anyone talked about what they wanted to do or be someday.

I'm happy to report she made it. And I have to admit that on her thirteenth birthday, we teased her quite a bit about the fact that she had already achieved her life's goal. What *was* she going to do with the rest of her life? I'm also happy to report that it didn't take long to for Olivia to realize that life had more to offer her than being a teenager and that she has grown up to do much more than turn thirteen.

As I think back to Olivia's life goal, I want to remind every parent of three lessons they need to learn from my sweet Olivia.

Lesson one: Respect your child's perception of goals and achievements—and even encourage them. To seven-year-old Olivia, turning thirteen seemed far away, but not so far that it was unreachable. It was also something she viewed as exciting and almost magical. In her eyes, to be thirteen was to be mature and independent. So when you look at it from that perspective, her goal was every parent's dream for their child.

Lesson two: Your children's goals for their lives need to be theirs…not yours. If your little one says he or she is going to be the president someday or is going to have a farm for animals no one wants, who are you to say they won't? Don't you think your child is smart enough or compassionate enough or good enough to accomplish what they set their hearts and minds to do? Besides, didn't *you* make *your* own choices?

Lesson three: *Never* dismiss your child's goals and dreams by making fun of them or by telling your child they are silly or impossible. That's like throwing the anchor out without having the other end of the rope tied to the boat. Trust me—this is not something you want to do. Your job as a parent is to instill hope and courage and self-confidence and the belief that they can do anything they set their mind to.

Someone once said that God gives us dreams a size too big so we can grow into them. Don't keep your children from growing. Their goals and dreams will likely change more times than you can count between now and the time they leave home. But even if they don't, your job is to love and build them up—not deflate them.

So while we did tease Olivia a bit, it was not to make fun of her or belittle her. Nor did we do so when she was too young to understand what we were saying and why. She and her siblings knew (and still do) that we believe they can do anything they set their hearts and minds to do. The question is...do your children know the same?

Love,
Momma D

But seek first his kingdom and his righteousness, and all these
things will be given to you as well.
~Matthew 6:33 (NIV)

Warning: Bad Mom-Moment Ahead

Our three oldest children were six, three, and one when we packed them up and took them from the tiny but happy place they called home and moved almost 200 miles away because of John's promotion and to breathe some life back into my family's farm. When all was said and done, life happened the way it was supposed to. God knew exactly what he was doing, and our family has been blessed beyond measure. But that doesn't mean the move was without its lumps and bumps and bruises. In fact, one of my biggest parent fails took place during this move.

Zach was six and just getting ready to enter first grade. Now when I say "just getting ready," I'm not exaggerating. We arrived in Rolla on Saturday evening, and the school year started on Monday. And if that wasn't enough upheaval for a six-year-old, our house/farm was far from being ready to occupy, so we spent the first six weeks living out of suitcases with Granny.

Spending so much time with Granny wasn't the problem, though. The problem was that not having our own home right away meant that in addition to leaving his home and his friends, Zach also had to leave behind our dog, Maggie, and his pony, Casey.

So where does the parent fail come in with all of this? Glad you asked. We were so focused on getting the house ready to live in, and John had a lot going on in transitioning into his new position, that we did not give Zach's feelings the compassion and TLC they deserved...or that he needed. I even remember talking to him about the fact that we had sold all our livestock, knowing it wasn't feasible to bring them. We said we would start over when fences were in place, barns were repaired, and so on. As if Maggie and Casey were no more important than cows in a field that could easily be replaced! Talk about a few *bad* mom moments! Ouch!

Nothing could change the fact that it simply wasn't possible to bring Maggie and Casey with us. But I could have handled it a *whole* lot better than I did.

I'd like to be able to tell you that was the only bad mom-moment I've had in my years of raising four children. But I can't— not truthfully, anyway. What I can say, however, is that from this experience, I learned that the feelings of little people matter—they matter a lot. What seems like a little thing to you and I can be breaking their little hearts into a million pieces. As parents, we need to take their feelings seriously—making them our own. We need to treat them with the love and care they deserve.

So *please,* never laugh at your child's feelings, never tell them it's no big deal or that they need to just get over it. Listen to them, let them share what is in their heart, let them cry, let them be angry, and then talk *with* them about how to make the situation better.

Love,
Momma D

Love must be sincere. Hate what is evil; cling to what is good.
Be devoted to one another in love. Honor one another above
yourselves. Never be lacking in zeal, but keep your spiritual
fervor, serving the Lord. Be joyful in hope, patient in affliction,
faithful in prayer.
~Romans 12:9-12 (NIV)

Mommy, Why Does Santa Like Some Kids More Than He Likes Me?

The other day at the beginning of the holiday season a couple of years ago, I read a letter from a mom to parents everywhere. The letter requested that parents not give their children expensive gifts in the name of Santa Claus. She asked that if parents felt the need to give their children expensive gifts at Christmastime, that they let their children know these things were from them, letting Santa give them the smaller, less expensive gifts.

The reason for her request was simple—she wanted her children (and millions of others like them) to feel just as loved and valued by Santa as those children who received bigger and better gifts from him.

You see, this mother's little girl came home from school the other day feeling less valued and loved than some of the other children in her class. It seems they had been discussing what Santa was going to be bringing, and several of the little girl's classmates were getting a whole lot more than she was. This momma's heart was breaking when the little girl said, "Does Santa like some kids more than he does others? Does he like _____ more than he likes me?"

When I read this, two things happened.

- My heart became heavy. It became heavy for this momma who was faced with trying to explain their lack of financial means. My heart was heavy for the little girl who was made to question her self-worth and who was already aware that to some (many), your value was measured in dollars and cents. My heart was heavy for everyone who was missing what the season is all about.
- I could relate. I remember putting a play kitchen on layaway and needing the entire three months to pay that sixty dollars. I remember putting gifts under the

tree every Christmas Eve after the kids went to bed while John asked, "Were we able to do it? Are they going to happy when they wake up and see what they got?"

But as I write this, I find myself recalling many memories of Christmases past, and I realize few of them are about the actual gifts I received. They were about the people and places I experienced Christmas with. I am blessed to have a lifetime of Christmas memories and family and friends who understand what Christmas is really all about, and it doesn't have a thing to do with money.

What message are you sending to your children this Christmas? Is it a message that says bunches of presents equals bunches of joy? Or is it a message that says the only present that really matters is one wrapped and given with love?

Love,
Momma D

Do not store up for yourselves treasures on earth, where moths and vermin destroy, and where thieves break in and steal. But store up for yourselves treasures in heaven, where moths and vermin do not destroy, and where thieves do not break in and steal. For where your treasure is, there your heart will be also.
~Matthew 6:19-21 (NIV)

The REAL Santa Knows What He's Doing

For the past several years I have had the esteemed honor of taking Mackenzie and Macy to see Santa...the *real* Santa. Seriously—this guy is the real deal right down to the long white beard and a kind, gentle smile and personality.

This year, though, while we were waiting in line to see him, Mackenzie said, "Nanna, he's going to ask Macy and I if we've been good, isn't he?"

"Yes," I said, "he is. And when he does, you can both tell him you are very good girls because you are two of the best girls in the whole entire world."

She listened to what I said, smiled her sweet smile with a look of relief in her eyes, hugged my leg, and turned back to the displays next to us meant to keep the kids occupied while they waited to meet Santa.

Mackenzie's question wasn't asked with a great deal of anxiety or dread, but it bothers me that we (we, meaning society in general) have placed the thought in our children's minds that Santa's goodness and generosity is performance-based. We've demoted Santa from the giver of love and good cheer to one who rewards only the good.

How sad is that! What's more, if a little child is worried about what a stranger in a red suit and beard thinks of them, what do you think goes through their heads and hearts when you make them feel like they've disappointed you and let you down? What impression are you leaving in their tender little hearts and impressionable little minds when you give the impression that your love and respect have to be earned?

Our children don't ask to be born. We make that decision for them. So the very least we can do is to let them know they don't have to earn our love any more than they should have to be good in order to have a present or two under the tree on Christmas morning.

Our wait to see Santa was relatively short, and both girls climbed up in his lap ready to tell him what they wanted. And you know what? Santa didn't ask if they'd been good. Instead, he smiled at the girls and said, "I can see you are both very sweet (not good) little girls, so tell me what you'd like for Christmas."

See, I *told* you he was the real deal.

Love,
Momma D

But the Lord said to Samuel, "Do not consider his appearance or his height, for I have rejected him. The Lord does not look at the things people look at. People look at the outward appearance, but the Lord looks at the heart."
~1ˢᵗ Samuel 16:7 (NIV)

My Dad Can Do a Cartwheel...Can Yours?

If you're a mom, there's a dad to go with you and vice versa. You may be raising your children as a single parent, or like me, you may be blessed with a parenting partner who has been active and present in all phases of your parenting journey, but either way you can't be a mom or dad without each other. It's simple biology.

Each week, I share something I've experienced and learned as a mom and nanna. But this week, I want to give credit to my parenting partner and love of my life, John.

John worked diligently and sacrificially as a law enforcement officer for thirty years, putting in long, stressful hours so that I could be a stay-at-home mom and wife. It's true, he wasn't always able to attend every school program, 4-H event, or church outing. And there were many nights he wasn't there to eat dinner with us or say good night before they went to bed. But as our youngest daughter Emma said a couple of years ago, "I get it now. Anytime Dad wasn't able to be there was simply so you could be, Mom."

John may not have been there for everything, but he was there for the really important things. He was there to help me bring each of our four children into the world. He was there to make memories on family camping trips. He was there to cheer Zach on at soccer games, cross country meets, and track meets. He was there to help the kids show their livestock at the fair. He was there to worship with them in church (unless he had to work). He was there when each of them accepted Christ as their Savior. He was to take them sledding, teach them how to work hard, discipline them, rescue them from runaway ponies and angry roosters, teach them why and how to choose between the microwave and the hoodie (that's another story for another day), to walk each of our daughters down the aisle, to stand up with our son on his wedding day, and to turn cartwheels in the living room and dance with his daughters to *Alvin and the Chipmunks Christmas Album*. But most of all, he was (and still is) there to show them what it is to be a man of integrity, honor, loyalty, and grace, and a man who loves the Lord.

The lesson I want to leave you with this week is this: No matter what condition your relationship with your children's father is in, parenting is a team effort. Children need both a mom and a dad. Your roles are different, yet the same. You both have a responsibility to make memories, discipline, invest yourselves into your children's lives, and love unconditionally.

Thank you, John, for parenting with me. I couldn't have done it without you!

Love,
Momma D

Start children off on the way they should go, and even when they are old they will not turn from it.
~Proverbs 22:6 (NIV)

What's Blue and Yellow, Made Out of Paper, and Seen Only Once a Year?

In early December of 1984, Zach, who was almost two, came walking out of his Sunday school class carrying a paper angel covered in blue and yellow crayon scribbles. The angel had a strip of paper on each side of the bottom of the skirt that had been taped together to form a circle. The purpose of this angel? To sit on the top of a Christmas tree.

When Zach proudly handed me the paper angel, I promised we would put it on top of the tree as soon as we got home and that it would sit on top of my Christmas tree forever (as long as I was living).

So would you like to guess what is sitting on top of my Christmas tree this year—just like every year beginning in 1984? That's right. It's the paper angel Zach made. Hey, I promised, and promises are meant to be kept.

When you make a promise to your children (or anyone, for that matter), you are putting your integrity on the line and are providing your children with the answer to the question of whether or not they can trust you...really trust you. When you keep your promises, your children see you as safe and trustworthy. Breaking your promises, however, is unsettling to your children. They feel exposed and vulnerable. They don't know when to trust you and when not to. If this happens very often, they will quit trusting you altogether. And when this happens, you lose their respect as well.

I made the promise to Zach that day because a) I wanted him to know how much I valued his efforts, b) I wanted to make him feel special, and c) I wanted to establish a tradition for our little family. I've kept the promise I made to Zach all those years ago because a) I want him to always know my word is good and he can trust me no matter what, and b) because I *love* that little paper angel.

Over the next few years, our little family doubled in size from three to six. Promises were made to each of the girls (and kept). More traditions were added along the way, as well, but none replaced the tradition of our paper tree angel because I promised, and promises are meant to be kept.

How well do you keep the promises you make to your children? Do you keep them, or do you promise things in an effort to gain compliance or a little peace and quiet? I hope you keep them because (in case you haven't picked up on it yet) promises are meant to be kept.

Love,
Momma D

I will not violate my covenant or alter what my lips have uttered.
~Psalm 89:34 (NIV)

Don't Spill Those Beans

A few weeks ago, I was playing game after game after game of *Don't Spill the Beans* with Mackenzie and Macy. If you aren't familiar with the game, allow me to give you a brief explanation...

Each person takes their turn placing a plastic bean on the bean pot balanced on two arms. The object of the game is to *not* spill the beans by upsetting the balance of the bean pot each time you place your bean in the pile. It's actually pretty fun. So much fun, in fact, that Mackenzie was barely able to wait her turn.

I can't even begin to count the number of times I said, "Not yet, Mack. It's Macy's turn." Or, "Not yet, Mack, it's my turn." Mackenzie wasn't trying to steal a turn. She was simply excited to be playing the game. She was enjoying herself so much that she was having a hard time waiting for her turn to come around again.

As I thought about this the next morning (when they asked to play again), I thought about how similar life is to Mackenzie's exuberance in playing *Don't Spill the Beans*.

Kids are in such a hurry to grow up. They don't want to wait their turn. It starts when they are toddlers wanting to stay up later. From there, it progresses to:

- Wanting to wear clothes that make them look older.
- Wearing makeup.
- Playing on competitive sports teams that expect you to practice for hours each week.
- Thinking they need a cell phone before they know how to carry on a conversation that goes beyond "Do you want to come over to my house and play?"
- Dating even though they can't drive.

And let's not forget this one—wanting to be treated as an adult before they even have a job.

As parents, it is your responsibility to not let your kids grow up too quickly. Kids have only eighteen years to be kids, and you need to make sure they make the most of those eighteen years.

I'm not saying children shouldn't be given chores to do or be expected to be responsible. And I'm not saying they should be babied and sheltered from anything and everything that causes them to ask questions and make choices. These things are all part of being a kid. What I am saying, though, is this: Don't allow (or expect) your kids to be older than they are. Don't let them add a bean to the pot before it's time and throw their life off balance.

Take it from me—the years really do pass too quickly. Your kids will be grown up and gone before you know it, so enjoy each moment and provide your kids with an environment that will allow them to do the same.

Love,
Momma D

When I was a child, I talked like a child, I thought like a child, I reasoned like a child. When I became a man, I put the ways of childhood behind me.
~1st Corinthians 13:11 (NIV)

Swallow That Apple

Last week, I was reminded of an incident (if you want to call it that) that took place over twenty-seven years ago. It wasn't anything big or dramatic, but like all those little things usually do, it holds a lesson for us all.

Picture it…five little ones sitting around a table eating their lunch. They were ages six, five, four, three, and eighteen or nineteen months. The four-year-old and one-and-a-half-year-old were mine—the other three were my friends' boys whom I took care of frequently.

Anyway…everyone was pretty much done, so I was wiping hands and faces before they left the table to play. Elizabeth, the one-and-a-half-year-old, however, obviously still had a mouthful of something. Upon further investigation, I discovered she was hoarding her diced up apple in her cheek like a chipmunk. Why? Who knows? But nothing I said or did could convince her to swallow that apple—not even threatening to take away her beloved Stacy (her doll).

Elizabeth held that cheek full of apple in her mouth for *hours*. I'm talking like four or five hours! Why? Again, who knows. But here is what I *do* know…

Kids hold on to a lot more than a mouthful of mushed-up apple. They hold on to memories of games played, stories read, and harsh words spoken and being ignored. They hold on to memories of favorite foods, favorite shirts, and being criticized for being chubby and looking sloppy or weird or whatever term was used. Kids hold on to memories of camping trips, picnics, the first fish they caught, and seeing the back of your head more than any other part of you because you were too busy working or taking time for yourself.

Are you holding on to what I'm putting out there for you to take hold of? I hope so, but I'm not done yet. There's a flip side to this coin. Sometimes kids hold on to things they need to let go of.

We parents are people, too. We're not perfect. So if you have a child who is holding on to the fact that you missed a school program—even though you didn't miss fifty-two others—don't let them make you feel guilty or use this as a weapon against you. Or if your child won't let go of the fact that your trust in them has been broken because of something they've done, don't let them use this to make you feel guilty or second-guess yourself. They are the ones that need to let it go and work toward rebuilding that trust.

Holding on to the right things can be great. It can even save your life. Holding on to the wrong things, however, can get you and your children hurt. So do your best to be the kind of parent who gives your child enough good things for them to fill their hands and arms with. In doing so, hopefully, they won't have any room left for the not-so-good things. Either way, if you do the best you can, you can go to bed each night knowing that you did just that—your best.

We'll never know why Elizabeth held on to that mouthful of apple all those years ago. Maybe it was to give me something to write about today.

Love,
Momma D

I praise you for remembering me in everything and for holding to the traditions just as I passed them on to you.
~1st Corinthians 11:2 (NIV)

I Am from Leftover Cookie Dough and Walnut-Stained Hands

Lately, I've found myself thinking about the house/farm we called home for all the years we were raising our kids. It was the same place my grandpa was born. It was the same place my mom was born. The roots ran true and deep, and there's no other place I would have wanted to raise my children.

The house you raise your family in and the effort you put into making it a home is vital to your child's sense of self-worth and confidence. But you might be surprised to learn that it's not the size of the house, the amenities of the house, or the address of the house that make it a home. To your children, it is the culmination of your family's fingerprints—the tangible and intangible personality traits that make the home—that builds your children into adults.

I could spend a few minutes expounding on what I mean by family fingerprints or personality traits, but instead, I'll let a small portion of Emma's poem—one she wrote in high school—do the job for me.

Where I Come From—by Emma Noble

I am the floor that creaks…
The red tile kitchen floor…
I am from 105.3 in my brother's first truck…
From the walnuts that stain my hands…
From the chair I stood on to dry dishes…
From my mom's flowerbeds, sidewalk chalk, gravel on my bare
_   feet…_
From a musty barn full of sheep…
I am leftover cookie dough…
I am from pigtails and cowboy boots to T-shirts and peace signs…
I am from the scar on my finger from sticking rocks in the VCR
_   when I was three…_

I am from Golden Girls reruns...
Never having to lock our doors...
From my sisters' clothes...
From red church pews—when churches still had pews...
The metal bowl in the kitchen and knowing what's in every
cabinet...
From my dad's hankie in his back pocket; he always has one...
I am from 12750 County Road 7160

Take it from Emma, parents, raising kids is about the little things...a whole lot of little things that make life something to smile about.

Love,
Momma D

Better a dry crust with peace and quiet than a house full of
feasting, with strife.
~Proverbs 17:1(NIV)

Quit Trying

For most of my life, I've been okay with the fact that I have naturally curly hair. In fact, I'm actually thankful for my hair...but it hasn't always been that way. You see, I was in junior high and high school when Farrah was in her prime; meaning you couldn't turn in any direction without seeing long, layered hair with feathered bangs that required a *lot* of hairspray to hold them in place. And if you didn't have that kind of hair, you had the short and very straight Dorothy Hamill look with that perfect little upsweep in the back that came to a point.

And then there was me...and Penny, Donna, and Lisa. Layers only made it curlier, feathered bangs were not an option (feathers aren't curly, you know), and the whole Dorothy thing, well, that was definitely out of the question.

So what did I do? I gave up, that's what! I gave up trying to transform myself into someone I wasn't. And you know what? I turned out just fine. I married my childhood sweetie (he loves my curls). I raised four nearly-perfect kids who have given me five absolutely perfect grandchildren. And I am honoring God by using my gift for writing to educate and encourage people around the world (hopefully, you're one of them).

The moral of this story is *QUIT TRYING*! Quit trying to make your eight-year-old into a musician when he/she would rather be drawing pictures or building robots. Quit trying to turn your thirteen-year-old into a future scholarship awardee for playing soccer when he/she would rather be blowing into a clarinet or making jewelry to sell to all her friends. In other words, *quit trying* to turn their curls into feathers.

When you encourage or even force your kids to work on their weaknesses instead of their strengths, you set them up for failure and a sense of poor self-worth. You are also wasting time they could be spending doing things that make them feel great about themselves, things that inspire them toward a bright future. Now

I'm not saying you shouldn't encourage your six-year-old to keep trying when it comes to reading or that your two-year-old shouldn't be encouraged to use the big girl/boy potty. What I'm saying is this: God made us all uniquely special, and as parents, it's our job to help our kids learn to let that uniqueness shine brighter than the north star—not try to fix what we think God could have done better.

Love,
Momma D

For just as each of us has one body with many members, and these members do not all have the same function, ⁵ so in Christ we, though many, form one body, and each member belongs to all the others. ⁶ We have different gifts, according to the grace given to each of us.
~Romans 12:4-6a (NIV)

The Funnel Cake Lesson

I was talking to my daughter Olivia on the phone the other day, and in the course of our conversation, she said that Reuben had tasted his first funnel cake over the weekend. She laughed as she told me about handing him a bite of what we all know is a rather plain-looking treat. This was especially true since it wasn't completely smothered in powdered sugar.

Reuben looked at it, and when Olivia prompted him to do so, he took a bite. She could tell by the look on his face that his expectations were low, but it took only a second or two for his expression to change and for him to begin saying, "Yum, Mommy, yuuuummmm."

Reuben's initiation into the world of funnel cakes came with a very important lesson—one every child needs to learn: everything is not as it seems. Reuben's initial expression told Olivia he was expecting the funnel cake to taste like bread or a pretzel because that's what it looked like. It didn't look like anything sweet he'd ever had before.

As parents, we need to be teaching our children the same lesson—that everything is not as it seems.

Being told no may seem like a bad thing at the time, even though it really is for their own good. Peers who aren't dressed in the latest and greatest may not seem like people they want to be friends with, but they are usually kinder, nicer, and more loyal than kids dressed in the latest and greatest. Just because it seems okay to go to a party when no parents are going to be home doesn't mean it is.

It may not seem to your child like you love them when you discipline them and don't give them everything they want, but later they'll realize just what an expression of love those things were.

Kids are kids—which means they have a kid's perception of things. They can't help it, and they shouldn't have to. That's what you're there for—to help them see things for what they really are by being a wise and loving parent who provides safe boundaries in which they can discover the world through hands-on experience, coming out of it with powdered sugar on their faces.

Love,
Momma D

This is what the Lord says, he who made the earth, the Lord who formed it and established it—the Lord is his name: 'Call to me and I will answer you and tell you great and unsearchable things you do not know.'
~Jeremiah 33:2-3 (NIV)

That's My Dad

I recently had the privilege of being present while my daughter pinned her husband's new rank on his uniform in a ceremony on the military base where they are stationed. My job was to make sure seventeen-month-old Essie didn't steal the show.

The ceremony took place outside, so while we were waiting for it to begin, we heard and saw several groups of soldiers and marines marching and shouting cadences. Essie clapped and jabbered along—watching with interest *and* familiarity.

Familiarity? Yes. Dwight and Emma make a conscious effort to make Essie aware of who and what her daddy is and to have respect and pride for her special lifestyle. Respect and pride? Can a seventeen-month-old little girl know these things? The ease with which she took everything in, and the fact that this usually busy, talkative toddler knew to be quiet during the ceremony told me she most definitely can. She is as proud as a toddler can be to be the daughter of a Marine and to be a member of the US military.

The point I want to make is this: Your children need to know who you are (besides Mom or Dad). Your children need to know how you spend your days in order to make their life…their meals…their clothes…their comfort possible. Your children need to know how other people see you—the accomplishments you've achieved and what you like to do (besides be a parent, of course). Your children need to know that they aren't the reason you come home a bit distracted or grumpy sometimes. But why? Good question. Your children need to know…

- So that they will have a better understanding of why you say some of the things you say and do some of the things you do. They need to know you value home as much as they do.
- So that your children will have a greater appreciation and respect for your time, your work schedule, and the sacrifices you make for your family.

- So that your children can be proud of who you are (because they really want to be).

Don't let your child's only perception of who you are be the parent who comes home grumbling and complaining after a rough day or the parent who brags about getting freebies that "they'll never miss" or that "they owe you." And most of all, don't be the parent whose children feel in the way or in second place (at best) because you eat, sleep, and breathe your job. Be the parent whose children know what you do for a living, take pride in the whole person you are, and who respect you for *all* of who you are and what you do.

Love,

Momma D

Fathers, do not exasperate your children; instead, bring them up in the training and instruction of the Lord.

~Ephesians 6:4 (NIV)

Don't Tell Them You're My Mom

The first summer Olivia was old enough to go to church camp for more than an overnight stay was also one of the weeks I was to be the camp mom in the girl's dorm. Olivia was used to me being her youth leader at church, but for some reason, she wasn't thrilled at the prospect of not being the only member of our family at camp that week. She even said she didn't want the people to know I was her mom (although most of them already did). I told her that would be fine—that I wouldn't talk to her unless I had to. And I really was fine with that. I understood her need for independence, and I certainly didn't want to embarrass her or make her feel like a baby. After all, she was eight years old!

By the end of the first full day of camp, she was coming to me just like she normally would. She even called out "Mom!" from across the blacktop play area to get my attention. The secret was out! Apparently, Olivia had decided I wouldn't embarrass her, so it was safe to let everyone who didn't already know, know who I was.

I hadn't thought about that week in years, but the other day I was reading through the book of Proverbs and found Proverbs 17:6 *Children's children are a crown to the aged, and parents are the pride of their children.*

We spend plenty of time teaching, hoping, and warning our children about how and why not to embarrass *us* in public, but this verse clearly states that we, as parents, are to be a source of pride to our children. In other words, we need to be just as careful to not embarrass our kids. This means no dressing like we're sixteen, no telling embarrassing stories about our kids (especially in front of them), no wiping food off their faces with spit (or anything else, for that matter), no showing baby pictures to their prom dates, and no disciplining them openly in front of their friends.

I'm not perfect, so I know there's a chance I embarrassed my kids a time or two, so Zach, Elizabeth, Olivia, and Emma, I'm sorry if I did. It was never intentional.

As for Olivia and I being able to do camp together...we spent fifteen more years going to camp together each summer, making many of our most memorable and precious mother/daughter memories there—memories we will never forget.

So you see, it is possible to enjoy spending time with your kids without embarrassing them.

Love,

Momma D

But Ruth replied, "Don't urge me to leave you or to turn back from you. Where you go I will go, and where you stay I will stay. Your people will be my people and your God my God."
~Ruth 1:16 (NIV)

Your Terms...Your Turf

Elizabeth was in third or fourth grade when she asked if she could invite a new friend to come over after school to play. "Sure," I said. "No problem." So on the day that was chosen, I picked the girls up from school and headed home, thinking this would be like any other play date.

It didn't take long, however, for me to pick up some negative vibes about this little girl. She was rude to Olivia when Olivia walked into the bedroom Elizabeth and her friend were playing in—the bedroom Olivia shared with Elizabeth. When she didn't stop, I poked my head in and reminded everyone to be nice.

My reminder went in one ear and out the other, though, and pretty soon Elizabeth's new friend was at it again. I called to Olivia and told her to give the girls some space, but before she had time to leave the room, both Elizabeth and her new friend were being rude and unkind to Olivia. I issued another warning and reminded Elizabeth that this was not the way she was to treat her sister. Both my warning and comment was met with the infamous eye roll from the little girl who was a guest in our home, and an argument from Elizabeth.

That was it. I simply announced that the play date was over and it was time for me to take our guest home. The girls knew how to tell time. They knew it really wasn't time, but Elizabeth was also smart enough to not argue, so they gathered her friend's things, we got into the car, took her home, and she was not invited back. And just in case you are wondering, Elizabeth was not allowed to go to her house to play, either. In fact, the friendship didn't last very long after that day.

Your child's friendships are one of the most difficult aspects of parenting to do well or right. And just so you'll know upfront, you are probably going to mess it up a time or two, but you still have to be proactive and vigilant. How? Glad you asked.

First, teach your children to be nice to everyone. Being nice means being polite and not speaking unkindly or being a bully. Even the most disruptive and naughty children deserve to be treated with kindness. But being nice to everyone doesn't mean your child should be friends with everyone.

Secondly, know your child's friends. You can do this by following my rule of *your terms…your turf.* In other words, get to know your child's friends by having them in your home or supervising/chaperoning events in other places. This allows you to see who your children are playing with, how disciplined these children are, and how well their family's core values line up with yours. The *your terms…your turf* rule also gives your child the opportunity to have friends from both similar and different backgrounds without worrying whether or not they will be negatively influenced, like in the case of Elizabeth's playdate-gone-bad.

Once you know a child, then you can be more comfortable with letting your children spend time in the care and supervision of other parents. Teaching children to follow this rule can also help when they get to be teens by providing them with a way to handle peer pressure in a positive manner.

Let's face it, though. There are some kids you don't want your children hanging out with (and for justifiable reasons). Just remember that the way a child dresses, where he/she lives, what his/her folks do for a living, and the color of someone's skin aren't justifiable reasons. Dishonesty, rudeness, defiance, and treating others unkindly…*those* are justifiable reasons for steering your children away from a relationship.

Love,
Momma D

No discipline seems pleasant at the time, but painful. Later on, however, it produces a harvest of righteousness and peace for those who have been trained by it.
~Hebrews 12:11 (NIV)

What Have You Learned from Your Children?

Elizabeth is both my first and my second. She is my first daughter, but my second child. She is also a child who has shown me that

- Sleep is not nice, but not essential. Hey, I'm still here, aren't I?
- A mother's heart feels like it will burst with joy at the sound of your child's tiny voice singing about Jesus at the top of her lungs.
- You can never have too much of your favorite color—in her case it was purple.
- There is no limit to the number of peanut butter and jelly sandwiches a child should be allowed to eat.
- Tiny little girls can dream big dreams *and* make them come true.
- What you say and how you say it are equally important.
- The T-shirt that says, "I'm a nurse...what's your superpower?" was made with her in mind.

And finally, she, along with her sisters has shown me that raising your daughters to be Godly women, wives, and moms is the best kind of mother/daughter relationship there is.

The question to you now is this: What lessons are you learning from your children?

Love,
Momma D

Everyone who quotes proverbs will quote this proverb about you: "Like mother, like daughter."
~Ezekiel 16:44 (NIV)

Un-Parenting Is Not Parenting

I'm not going to go into any details, but it's safe to say that all four of my amazing and wonderful children went through stages of thinking they were wiser and more capable of making choices and decisions than they actually were. Once upon a time, I did the same thing. But hey, that's the nature of a teenager, isn't it? Of course it is! That's why the article I read yesterday was so troubling to me…and I hope to you as well.

The article was about *unschooling* your children—a supposedly up-and-coming method of education. So what is unschooling? Unschooling is letting your children discover the world on their own terms by following their instincts and doing what they feel passionate about. Oh, and if they happen to learn how to spell, construct a proper sentence, and know the significance of December 7, 1941 and October 29, 1929, well then, that's just the icing on the cake!

Please, oh, please, tell me you see how ridiculous—how wrong—this is! If I had taken that approach to my children's education, two of them wouldn't know how to read a price tag because for a few years they were convinced math was from the devil, another one of my kids would most likely have stopped reading once they got past the Dr. Seuss stage, two or possibly three of them would have spent most of their waking hours in the barn or playing outside, and I'm almost certain none of them would have bothered learning about the table of elements or how and why your heart beats and your food digests.

In case there's any doubt about how I feel about unschooling, let me just say this: unschooling is poor parenting. You may as well call it un-parenting. Unschooling cheats your child out of learning things they are incapable of accessing on their own. Unschooling puts your child in danger because they don't always have the ability to make sound, rational decisions. Unschooling removes boundaries from children—boundaries they will test, but boundaries they want and need to feel secure and loved. But most of all, unschooling sends the message that you don't feel your children are worth the effort it takes to invest yourself in them and to give them every opportunity to learn all they can about a variety of different things.

Instead of turning your children out to fend for themselves, you must provide structured education and clearly defined boundaries and expectations and give them the opportunity to discover and use what they are passionate about and explore the world on their terms through play time. Did I just say play time? Yes, I did. I said it because raising happy, healthy, well-adjusted children is all about that balance.

Love,
Momma D

How much better to get wisdom than gold, to get insight rather than silver!
~Proverbs 16:16 (NIV)

Do You Have a Salamander? Well, You Should!

Among the *many* pets our kids had over the years, one of my favorites was Sally the Salamander and the salamanders that came after her. Why? Oh, let me count the ways...

Sally and friends were low-maintenance and easy to care for. Sally and friends were friendly and nonaggressive. Sally and friends were hardy and didn't go to pet heaven at the drop of a hat.

Sally and friends were cute. Yes, cute. Something shiny black with bright yellow spots is cute no matter how you look at it.

But most of all, Sally and friends served as excellent reminders of what home and family are really all about. How? Glad you asked...

Salamanders live and thrive only where the ecosystem is perfectly balanced. This served to remind me that my children needed a balance of fun, laughter, freedom, rules, discipline, and times to be serious.

No two salamanders have the exact same spot pattern, reminding me that all four of my kids are different and need to be respected, loved, and appreciated for those differences. This fact also served to help me instill in my children that they are beautiful and uniquely created by God...and God don't make no junk.

Salamanders have the ability to grow new tails and even limbs. What a relief this has been to me at times when I've been a less-than-stellar parent when it comes to disciplining my kids or letting them know how precious they are to me. It reminds me that despite my imperfections, as long as my kids know my love for them is unconditional and unwavering, they are resilient and recover from my screwups.

Salamanders aren't aggressive, and they don't bully other animals, but they do have the subtle ability to protect themselves from predators by emitting a slimy coating over their bodies that is obnoxious to animals that try to attack them. While I never wanted or encouraged my kids to pick a fight or be a bully or mean girl, we gave them the skills and permission to stand up for themselves and to protect themselves from the emotional and physical assaults that came their way.

Salamanders lead a simple, quiet life. They live in humble settings and eat only what they need. Oh, and they return to the same pond to breed and lay their eggs year after year after year. I hope and pray I gave my children hearts that desire to live simply and without a sense of entitlement or hunger for money and things, and to be committed to family like Sally and friends were.

Who would have thought the lowly, silent salamander had so much to say?

I guess that leaves me with just one question for you: Do you have a salamander? If not, you should.

Love,
Momma D

Now if the foot should say, "Because I am not a hand, I do not belong to the body," it would not for that reason stop being part of the body. And if the ear should say, "Because I am not an eye, I do not belong to the body," it would not for that reason stop being part of the body. If the whole body were an eye, where would the sense of hearing be? If the whole body were an ear, where would the sense of smell be? But in fact God has placed the parts in the body, every one of them, just as he wanted them to be. They were all one part, where would the body be? As it is, there are many parts, but one body.
~1st Corinthians 12:15-20 (NIV)

The Day X Really Did Mark the Spot

When Emma was four, her favorite book was *Look Out for Pirates*. It's a story about a group of sailors who outwit some pirates, keeping them away from their treasure. And like all good pirate/buried treasure stories, X marks the spot. And let me tell you, Emma spent a bit of time hunting around the fields on our farm for an X.

It just so happens that on the far end of the lake where we spend a good deal of time, there is a small island. The outer edges are sand and gravel—perfect for a picnic, sunbathing, and resting after swimming. The inner part of the island, however, is filled with trees and underbrush. So...John and I decided to take the kids up there one day to swim and have lunch...and to finally give Emma the opportunity to find buried treasure.

Once we'd tied the boat off and were on the shore, John sneaked off to bury a little bag containing candy, gum, some money, and a few other little things. It wasn't buried very deep, and on top of it, he placed a great big X made from sticks. He was back in no time and suggested that we cut through the trees to go to the other side of the island. The kids were all game for that, so off we went with John leading the way, making sure Emma was closest to him. As we came to the place where X marked the buried treasure, John stopped, pretending he needed to blow his nose or something like that. It didn't take but a second for Emma to spy the X, and in no time, she had unearthed the buried treasure. She was overjoyed, to say the least, and thankfully her siblings, who quickly caught on, didn't blow our cover. In fact, they went right along with us, making the event even more special.

Now I know there may be some pragmatics out there thinking it was wrong to lie to Emma. But I don't agree. What we did for Emma that day was allow her to take an adventure she wanted to take. But we also did something else—something even more important. We showed Emma that even the seemingly impossible is possible—if you keep trying and don't give up.

It was a few years before Emma realized how the treasure came to be there that day, but that didn't matter to her. What mattered was that 1) it had been there, and 2) we valued her feelings enough to give her the experience.

The reminder I want to leave with you is this: Don't squelch your child's imagination and dreams. If you can help make your young child's dreams come true and allow them to live out some of their imagination (to an extent), you will find that as they grow older, your child won't be afraid to be their own individual rather than merely going with the flow. They will be more creative and confident.

So ask yourself: How can you help your child find their buried treasure?

Love,
Momma D

For nothing will be impossible for God.
~Luke 1:37 (NIV)

Great Expectations…No, Not the Book

My youngest granddaughter, Essie, is not yet two years old, but even at such a young age, she already knows—no, she expects—that her daddy will be on the other end of the phone whenever she picks up a play phone or her momma's cell phone. She picks it up, says, "Hi, Dada," and then proceeds to kiss the phone before saying "Bye." Essie also expects to see Nanna (that's me) whenever she passes by the computer and calls my name—thanks to Skype—and she expects to be happily satisfied when she bites into a boo boo (that's two-year-old for blueberry).

Essie's expectations stem from what she's seen and done in the past. It happened before so, in her mind, it should happen again and again.

Your children are no different. They have expectations for things to be the same…to be consistent. Consistency equals safety and security in their world. This is especially true when it comes to you. How consistent are you?

- Do you expect your children to comply with the same guidelines, rules, and expectations at home and in public?
- Do you expect your child's guests to comply with house rules rather than letting them get by with things you won't let your own children get by with?
- Do you parent consistently, giving your children the confidence that they can expect you to be the same no matter what day of the week it is?

On more than a few occasions, I've seen a parent reach for their child to put on a hat, zip a coat, wipe a face, or something similar, only to have the child flinch and recoil. There's only one reason for that—their expectation was that they were going to be hit.

Now while I am not at all opposed to a swat on the behind or on little hands reaching for things they shouldn't have, being slapped or hit by a parent should never be the normal expectation of any child.

I hope and pray Essie and my other sweet grandchildren never have these kinds of expectations. I hope and pray your children don't, either.

Love,
Momma D

My son, if sinful men entice you, do not give in to them.
~Proverbs 1:10 (NIV)

Sometimes They Did...Sometimes They Didn't...But They Always Survived

Can you smell it? You know...the smell of new crayons, glue sticks, new tennis shoes, and unsharpened pencils. Oh, the days of shopping for school supplies.

With four kids, it was quite an undertaking, and let's just say Wal-Mart was glad to see me coming. But I didn't mind. In fact, I had as much fun watching and helping them pick out what they needed and wanted (within reason) as they did. There's just something about starting something new that gives you energy and hope.

The kids hoped they got certain teachers. Sometimes they did...and sometimes they didn't.

The kids hoped they were in the same homeroom as their best friends. Sometimes they were...and sometimes they weren't.

The kids hoped their school ID pictures would look halfway decent instead of like a mug shot. Sometimes they did...and sometimes, well, you know the drill.

With each new school year came both excitement and disappointments. But then life is like that, isn't it?

After all, it's really not the end of the world if they don't always get the teacher they wanted. They're still going to learn what they are supposed to learn. And the world really won't stop turning if your child isn't in the same homeroom or lunch period as their best friend—I promise. The ID pictures? Sorry, no guarantee on that one, either. I mean is there anyone who can take a good picture when you have all of ten seconds to step into place and say cheese before the weird guy behind the camera takes one shot and hollers "Next!"?

As parents, we know these things aren't worth stressing over, but our kids don't—not yet anyway. That's where you come in.

It's your job to teach them to take things as they come and make the best of them—to instill in your children a sense of resiliency.

Children who are resilient have better social skills, have a stronger sense of self-confidence, are less likely to be bullied or to be a bully, and have stronger coping skills when it comes to things that really should be considered a struggle or disappointment. What's more, studies show that resilient children turn into resilient adults.

So...as the new school year approaches, don't feel bad about telling your child they have to choose a fifteen-dollar backpack instead of a $50 one. And don't let them whine and moan because they have first lunch period instead of third like *everyone* else does. They'll get over it...and be better people for it.

Love,
Momma D

Keep your lives free from the love of money and be content with what you have, because God has said, "Never will I leave you; never will I forsake you."
~Hebrews 13:5 (NIV)

Just Let Me Off Here

Zach was in the morning kindergarten class. This meant that each day around noon, Bob the bus driver would stop at the end of our driveway, bringing my little guy back home. One day, though, the bus didn't come at its usual time. I didn't think too much about it at first—probably because I had a two-year-old and a three-month-old to occupy my time. But when the bus was nearly thirty minutes late, I started to worry.

I called the school to see if they knew what was going on. They said yes, the bus was running late because they had a substitute driver who wasn't familiar with the route (which covered quite a bit of rural area). They assured me everything was fine and that Zach would be home in a matter of minutes.

Well, that matter of minutes turned into an additional thirty, and then forty-five. Still no Zach. I was really starting to panic. Where was my son???? I called John, who was working, and told him what the situation was. He called the school, got the same story, then called me back and assured me everything was fine. I looked at the clock and realized Zach was nearly two hours late. Things were *not* fine.

I was picking up the phone to call the school yet again when I saw Zach walking down the driveway. Relieved doesn't even begin to express what I felt at that moment, but when Zach told me what had happened, relief made room for anger.

The school was correct—the substitute driver didn't know the route and was aimlessly driving around asking these little ones where they lived. The problem was he never came down our road. Zach got so tired of riding, that after driving by the house of some friends of ours, he decided he could find his way home. So he told the bus driver to let him off—that our driveway was close by— and the bus driver did! Without a house or driveway in sight on a chilly November day, this man opened the door, let my six-year-old son out, and drove away—leaving Zach a little more than two miles from home!

Zach was a bit tired from his walk, but more than that, he couldn't believe "what a bad driver that man was." When I asked Zach how he knew the way home, he matter-of-factly told me he'd seen Colby's house and knew which way to go from there because we'd walked that way with him while he rode his pony a few times.

Now I know some of you may think we should have disciplined Zach for getting off the bus, but we didn't. We did talk to him about the fact that it would have been better for him to tell the bus driver how to get to our house instead of just getting off. The truth of the matter is that we were proud of Zach's confidence and awareness of his surroundings, and thankful for the fact that we lived in a rural community where he felt (and was) safe.

I'm not suggesting you turn your kids loose and let them wander at will without supervision—not at all! What I *am* saying, though, is that you need to make it a priority to ensure sure your kids are familiar with their surroundings, that they know a few different routes to your house, and that they know what places on these routes are safe places. Yes, I know the world is a scary place and that lots of bad things happen, but instead of over-sheltering your children and making them afraid, keep your children safe by protecting them *and* by teaching them to be strong, independent, and aware.

Love,
Momma D

Impress them on your children. Talk about them when you sit at home and when you walk along the road, when you lie down and when you get up. Tie them as symbols on your hands and bind them on your foreheads. Write them on the doorframes of your houses and on your gates.
~Deuteronomy 6:7-9 (NIV)

Chiggers...Blackberry Picking...Camping Trips...Arguments...and More

Parenting is about so much more than diapers, Band-Aids, homework, and curfews. Parenting is being there—listening, talking, forgiving, asking forgiveness, and most of all, loving unconditionally. I know this to be true because Momma D says it is.

These are the words directly under the title of this blog. These are my words. These are words I believe with all my heart. I also believe that to be this kind of parent, you have to experience life with your kids—the good, the bad, the funny, the sad, the beautiful, and the ugly...all of it.

Camping, putting up hay, mission trips, swimming, working in the greenhouse, crossing the finish line—these are some of the good experiences of life I've lived with my children.

Being covered in chiggers after picking blackberries, arguing and fighting over things that really don't matter, having to let them make their own mistakes—these are some of the bad experiences of life I've lived with my children.

Scaling rock cuts in sandals and nice clothes to catch runaway livestock, "saving" one of my kids from the beady-eyed stare of a vulture, countless games of hide-n-seek and program practices at church, farmer's markets and spending time at the fair—these are just a few of the fun and humorous experiences I've lived with my children.

Saying good-bye to Granny, leaving the friends, home, and pets we loved, burying beloved pets, hurting each other's feelings—these are some of the sad experiences of life I've lived with my children.

Giving birth to each of my children, watching my daughter as she helped care for Granny without complaining, sharing in each of my children's wedding day, being there to welcome each grandchild into our family's world, helping each child grow to be the person they are, watching each child take their own steps to become who they are—these arc the some of the beautiful experiences of life I've lived with my children.

Making mistakes, missed opportunities, unspoken words, being too busy…these are some of the ugly experiences of life I've lived with my children.

Remember…parenting is listening, talking, forgiving, asking forgiveness, being present, knowing when to act and when not to, and most of all, *LOVING*. So…unless you experience the good, bad, happy, sad, beautiful, and ugly of life *with* children, you cannot truly know who your children are and cannot be a parent who knows what it is to parent from the heart.

Love,
Momma D

If I speak in the tongues of men or of angels, but do not have love, I am only a resounding gong or a clanging cymbal. If I have the gift of prophecy and can fathom all mysteries and all knowledge, and if I have a faith that can move mountains, but do not have love, I am nothing. If I give all I possess to the poor and give over my body to hardship that I may boast, but do not have love, I gain nothing. Love is patient, love is kind. It does not envy, it does not boast, it is not proud. [5] It does not dishonor others, it is not self-seeking, it is not easily angered, it keeps no record of wrongs. Love does not delight in evil but rejoices with the truth. It always protects, always trusts, always hopes, always perseveres. Love never fails.
~1st Corinthians 1:1-8 (NIV)

Caution: Christmas Carolers NOT Welcome

Each holiday season, I naturally think back on special memories of things I've done with my family and those kids I call mine from the many years spent as a youth director at church. There are literally enough memories to fill a book (or two), but one that is particularly special because it still makes me laugh is one that involves caroling and a nursing home.

It was Saturday morning, and the other youth director and I were taking a fairly good-sized group of elementary and middle-school kids caroling at the nursing homes in our community. The first stop we made was to the home where a couple of our elderly church members were living, so we planned to make their rooms our first stop. But when we walked into the building, we found the lobby full of residents, so we decided to brighten their morning with our cheery voices. And so we sang. We sang *Up on the Housetop, Joy to the World, Rudolph the Red-Nosed Reindeer, Silent Night* and of course, we finished with a hearty rendition of *We Wish You a Merry Christmas.*

As soon as we finished the last note of our final song, one of the women in the room who was sitting in front of the television, turned to the woman sitting next to her and said (in a loud voice), "I'm glad those *$*# kids stopped singing. I couldn't hear the television."

I am laughing as I write because I can still see the looks of shock on their faces, immediately followed by one-syllable comments of "What?", "Huh?", and "Uhhhh" which were then followed by pursed lips trying to hold in giggles. It didn't work. But that was probably because I was laughing, too. We quickly regained our composure and left the room to sing for those we felt sure would be more appreciative. As we walked down the hallway, the kids started talking about what had happened...

"Did she really mean that?"

"No, I don't think so. Old people are just like that sometimes."

"Why didn't she like our singing?"

"Who knows? Maybe she has bad memories of Christmas, or maybe she's sad because no one comes to see her."

"Or maybe she's just a grouch."

"Maybe...probably."

"You think?"

"Oh, well, we didn't mean to make her mad. Besides, it's the thought that counts."

"That's right. We meant well."

They meant well. Their intentions were as pure as pure could be—to bring joy to elderly people at Christmas time—and no matter how it was perceived by some (or one), that really was what mattered. After making sure they understood they had done nothing wrong and that one person's response should not keep them from trying to make people smile, we continued caroling and had a great time doing so.

But as I think about that day now, I also think about how many times as parents we take our children's actions at face value rather than looking at the heart of the matter and their intentions.

When they cook breakfast and set the toaster on fire, do we only see burned toast or do we see an act of service out of love?

When we have to corral a runaway llama, do we see a hassle or do we see a child who was trying to do extra chores because she wanted to help out more? (My kids know what I'm talking about.)

When the orange towels bleed onto white T-shirts, do we see a child who is trying to do more than he is capable of or do we see a child trying to help out while you are sick in bed with the flu?

Are you getting the message here?

Our children are not perfect. Sometimes they make messes and mistakes in the process of doing something with the purest and best of intentions to help...serve...love.

The question is this: Do we see past the mess and into their heart, or do we leave the impression that we are just waiting for our children to stop singing so we can hear the television?

Love,
Momma D

Whatever you do, work at it with all your heart, as working for the Lord, not for human masters.
~Colossians 3:23 (NIV)

Way to Finish!

If you spend any time at all around children, you know they can be incredibly sweet and incredibly mean in the time it takes for the heart to beat another beat. They don't always mean to be mean. Sometimes it just happens. You know what I'm talking about—one toddler takes another toddler's toy, and within seconds you have an all-out toy room brawl on your hands. Or when someone makes fun of your second grader's haircut, they strike back out of the need to mask their hurt and humiliation.

There comes a time, however, when these outbursts of meanness are no longer reflexes or innocent acts of self-preservation. There comes a time when children mistreat others because they want to...because it gives them a sense of power...because they think it is okay to make fun of someone else...because they can. But parents, hear me loud and clear when I say it is *never ever* okay for your child to make fun of someone, and it is your job as a parent to teach and reinforce this essential life lesson.

I've said it before, and I'll say it again—I'm far from being the perfect parent, but this is one of the things I know I got right. All four of my children demonstrated this on numerous occasions, but one of the most vivid recollections of this comes from my son, Zach.

Zach was a runner—both track and cross country. No, Zach was a *really good* runner. He broke school records and was awarded numerous gold, silver, and bronze medals that proved his skill. Had they awarded medals for good sportsmanship and teamwork, Zach would have earned gold in those, too. You see, there was a boy on Zach's track and cross country teams who was looked at as strange...odd...nerdy...or whatever similar word you would like to insert there. He was the kid no one sat with at lunch,

75

the one who got his books knocked out of his hands, and experienced all those ridiculous, mean-spirited high school shows of immaturity. On top of that, this boy consistently finished last. Dead last. But each and every time this boy came across the finish line, he did so with Zach cheering him on, clapping, encouraging, and saying, "Way to finish, Forrest."

Zach and I never really talked about why he did it, but I knew. He did it because he knew it was the right thing to do. He knew this young man deserved to feel valued and respected for finishing. Yes, he may have always finished last, but he always finished, and Zach knew what it took to do so.

Teaching your children to see life through the eyes of others— especially those they see as fodder for ridicule, humiliation, pranks, and bullying—is a gift to everyone and a valuable lesson in compassion, honor, and integrity.

I'm sure Zach wasn't always a gold medalist in the way he treated others. In fact, I'm sure his sisters would vouch for that. Hey, no one is perfect. But I am sure he knows it is never okay to be a bully and that everyone deserves to be treated fairly and with kindness.

With all the pressure put on kids today to be the best...at the top of the heap...number one...to look just so...and all the other junk society throws at them, it can be difficult for them to understand that it is *not* okay to mistreat others and that winning at all costs is *not* okay.

As a parent, you must teach and model behavior that says just the opposite—that treating others the way you want to be treated is what life is really all about.

Love,
Momma D

For this very reason, make every effort to add to your faith goodness; and to goodness, knowledge; and to knowledge, self-control; and to self-control, perseverance; and to perseverance, godliness; and to godliness, mutual affection; and to mutual affection, love. For if you possess these qualities in increasing measure, they will keep you from being ineffective and unproductive in your knowledge of our Lord Jesus Christ.
~2nd Peter 1:5-8 (NIV)

One Fish, Two Fish Says I'm Just So Mad that Olivia is in London to Visit the Queen while the Berenstain Bears Have a House in Bear Country

For Zach, it was *One Fish, Two Fish, Red Fish, Blue Fish* and his Children's Bible (particularly Daniel and the Lion's Den and Balaam's Donkey).

Elizabeth's favorites were Richard Scarry's *Best Word Book Ever* and Mercer Mayer's *Little Critter* books.

Olivia never tired of *A House is a House for Me* and *Mother Goose Rhymes*—especially "Pussycat, Pussycat..." because I always exchanged the word *pussycat* for *Olivia*.

Reading *Hattie and the Fox* was a multiple-times-a-day event for Emma, along with any and all of the *Berenstain Bears* books.

The repetition of reading the same books over and over and over and over and (take a deep breath) over again was not always my favorite thing to do, but I did it because it made them happy, and I wanted my kids to be happy. But more than that, the repetition of hearing their favorite stories multiple times a day gave them a sense of security and belonging.

That's what repetition does, you know. It gives children a sense of belonging and assurance that things are just as they should be. And that is why, as a parent, you need to make sure you consistently and repeatedly

Tell your children you love them—every single day.

Make sure your actions are affirmations of what you say—Kids are smart. They know the difference between empty words and words giving voice to acts of love.

Keep the promises you make—If you can't keep them, don't make them.

Pick them up on time—Be where you say you will be when you say you will be there. Children are frightened and humiliated when you are late or miss something altogether.

Practice what you preach—Again, kids are better at spotting a phony than they are at addition or subtraction. They need to see you consistently and repeatedly being the person you tell them to be.

I've not been a perfect parent, but I've been consistent and repetitive in loving, protecting, nurturing, teaching, and caring for my children. I hope and pray you will do the same.

Love,

Momma D

PS I can *still* quote most of these books by heart, and I wouldn't have it any other way.

Children are a heritage from the Lord,
offspring a reward from him.
~Psalm 127:3 (NIV)

My Perfectly Wonderful Imperfect Life

As I write this, I am watching the movie, *Mom's Night Out*. If you have seen the movie, you know what I'm talking about when I say God love 'em. If you haven't seen the movie, you should.

As I watched, I was reminded of a time that seems like only yesterday when Granny was always putting Olivia's shoes on the right feet when we got to church because I couldn't seem to get it done. But hey, we were always on time, and all four kids were always dressed appropriately.

As I watched, I was reminded of the time I asked five-year-old Zach to check to see if baby Olivia was still sleeping, and he returned with her in his arms...after changing a cloth diaper because she was wet. He was smiling from ear to ear and said, "Don't worry, Mommy, I did not poke her."

As I watched, I was reminded of the gazillion toys I picked up off the floor, the spelling lists practiced, the stories read, the school parties and field trips chaperoned, the Halloween costumes made, the Easter eggs dyed and hidden, and all the other things moms do.

As I watched, I was reminded of the handmade cards, the fact that I still use the pin cushion Elizabeth made from fabric in Granny's scrap basket, the spaghetti dinner the girls made and served to John and me one year on our anniversary, the picture and note of apology handcrafted by Emma when she accidently let the llama out of the field. Yes, we had a llama. Doesn't everyone?

Our refrigerator was always covered in drawings and notes from school. There were always at least six pairs of shoes at the back door. I rarely went to ladies meeting at church without the kids in tow (John worked a lot of night shifts), and for several years our tax returns were our yearly contributions to the orthodontist.

Our life was loud and busy. The house was always clean, but often messy. I wore out three washing machines in twenty years, and we didn't bother keeping the wood floors waxed because they were needed for tap dancing and gymnastic stunts. And I wouldn't change a thing!

Being a parent is the most important job in the world. No exceptions. As a parent, you are giving the world an extension of yourself. To be a parent is to shape the future of society. No small task, I think you'll agree. So the next time you find yourself at your wit's end, craving five minutes of peace, questioning your sanity, wondering if it will ever be your turn to do something for yourself or feeling like a complete failure, stop. Stop and realize that the hand that rocks the cradle really does rule the world.

Love,
Momma D

*She watches over the affairs of her household and does not eat
the bread of idleness. Her children arise and call her blessed;
her husband also, and he praises her.
~Proverbs 31:27-28 (NIV)*

Momma, Why Does Granny Have a Screensaver?

Emma was in kindergarten the year Granny had surgery to replace one of her heart valves. I understand these two events wouldn't normally be linked together, but in this case, I think you will agree with me that they do.

The evening before the surgery was spent with Granny in her hospital room talking, reassuring one another, and even cracking several jokes about the fact that the valve she would receive would either be courtesy of a cow or a pig.

I noticed Emma didn't say much, but I didn't think too much about it because a) I knew she was worried about her granny, and b) Emma wasn't a chatty little girl. She was my quiet, contemplative one.

Of course she was quiet. There was a lot to take in and try to process. So I made a mental note to myself to give her a little extra reassurance before tucking her into bed that night. But as it turns out, Emma was making sense of things the way kids growing up in this day and age would.

As we were walking to our car after telling Granny goodnight, Emma looked up at me and asked, "Momma, why does Granny have a screensaver?"

"What?" I asked.

"Why does Granny have a screensaver?"

It took me a few seconds to figure out what she was talking about, but then it hit me—Emma thought Granny's heart monitor was a computer! Thankfully I was smart enough not to laugh at her. Instead, I agreed that the monitor looked like a computer (as she understood a computer to be), but I told her it was really a machine that was watching over Granny's heart.

We've laughed about this several times since then, but today I want to use this little incident to remind you to not deprive your children of the fun that can be had and the simple joys of life not associated with a computer in any of its various forms. Or as Miranda Lambert sings…

Hey, whatever happened to waitin' your turn
Doing it all by hand,
'Cause when everything is handed to you
It's only worth as much as the time put in
It all just seemed so good the way we had it
Back before everything became automatic.

So here is my challenge to you:

- Don't allow phones or other devices at the dinner table
- Make it clear that texting one another while in the same house is never acceptable
- Write messages to your children using paper and pen
- Help your little ones write cards and letters to their grandparents and encourage your older children to do the same
- Play *board* or *card* games as a family—not video games
- Cook together…from scratch
- Have a sixties or seventies weekend at home—doing things the way they did back then
- Spend one Saturday a month working together or learning a skill that requires you to do things by hand (woodworking, gardening, embroidery, crochet, baking, etc.)

While each generation makes both positive and negative contributions to society, we've allowed most of the positives from the past to become nearly extinct. Let's bring a few of them back, okay, because children need to know that not everything revolves around hard drives, apps, and the cloud.

Love,

Momma D

All Scripture is God-breathed and is useful for teaching, rebuking, correcting and training in righteousness, so that the servant of God may be thoroughly equipped for every good work.
~2nd Timothy 3:16-17 (NIV)

Just You and Me

One Fourth of July weekend, our entire family spent a few days with my in-laws and some of our extended family. The days were spent swimming, boating, eating, talking... I guess you could sum it up by saying a good time was had by all.

At one point, several of us—including my six-year-old granddaughter, Mackenzie—were sitting outside on the deck talking. Then for a variety of reasons, everyone but Mackenzie and I went back inside. As soon as we were alone, she jumped up from her chair, climbed up onto my lap, gave a big sigh, and said, "Finally, Nanna, it's just you and me." This, of course, was followed by some snuggle time and conversation about Two-Socks the horse, Bonnie the dog, and first-grade learning experiences.

Mackenzie's relief at it being just the two of us wasn't rude or unkind. She loves her grandpa, her aunts and uncles, great-grandparents and cousins. She also thoroughly enjoys spending time with older second cousins who aren't so old that they think a six-year-old is completely annoying. No, Mackenzie just needed some one-on-one time with her nanna—the very same kind of personal time your kids and/or grandkids need from you.

You may be thinking it's hard enough to get everyone where they're supposed to be on time while trying to get everyone's laundry washed and put away, keep the house picked up and meals cooked, and all the other necessary things required of you to keep everyone's lives up and running. But think about this...your family won't be a family if its members aren't loved and cherished and made to feel special. Instead, you'll be nothing more than a group of people surviving together under the same roof.

That's why it is important to spend time with each child—talking just to them, praying just with them, playing a game just with them, doing chores and fun projects just with them, going on a "date" just with them. To do so will give each child the validation they need and deserve and allow you to really *know* your child as a person.

It's like a jigsaw puzzle—even when the pieces are in the box or scattered on the table, it's still a puzzle. But when you take the time to carefully look at each piece enough to know exactly how and where it fits, those pieces become part of something everyone can enjoy.

Trust me, it's soooooooo worth the time you don't *think* you have—both for you and your children. I know this to be true, because a few weeks ago my daughter, Olivia, left Matt and Reuben at home overnight so she could spend the night with me and help me with a project the next day. As we sat in the restaurant enjoying dinner (just the two of us), she said, "I love it when we're all together, but I really miss not having it be just you and me like we used to."

I guess I'm going to have to do something about that, aren't I?

Love,
Momma D

Two are better than one, because they have a good reward for their toil. For if they fall, one will lift up his fellow. But woe to him who is alone when he falls and has not another to lift him up! Again, if two lie together, they keep warm, but how can one keep warm alone? And though a man might prevail against one who is alone, two will withstand him—a threefold cord is not quickly broken.
~Ephesians 4:9-12 (NIV)

I'm an Inside GIRL

Like most preschoolers, Macy doesn't have an external volume control. Okay, let's just tell it like it is—unless she decides to do so, she has no volume control. That was especially true one rainy day when we were stuck inside and getting bored.

Macy and Mackenzie were pretending to be horses and cowgirls. That was great, but the noise level just kept getting louder and louder. When I told them to quiet down, Macy didn't get the message (or couldn't hear it), so I said, "Macy, use your inside voice."

"I'm not an inside boy, Nanna, I'm an inside *girl*," she shot back with a confused and hurt look on her face. How dare I call her a boy!

Me: "No, honey, I said use your inside *voice*."

Macy (getting perturbed): "Nanna, I am not an inside boy! I'm an inside *girl*!"

Me (laughing): "Macy, I know you're a girl. I was telling you to talk in a quiet voice."

Macy (smiling): "Oh, okay."

And she did...for a little while, at least. Macy Scout isn't the only child to misunderstand what was said to her, to hear something completely different than what was actually said or intended. But often these misunderstandings aren't nearly as simple to fix...or funny.

When you say "No, not *that* way," your child hears "You can't do anything right." When you say "Why can't you be like...," your child hears "You aren't good enough." When you say "I don't have time," your children hear "You are not a priority." When you say...well, hopefully, you get the picture.

I know firsthand that sometimes our children don't get the right message even when we say everything in the right way—as was the case with Macy Scout. But more often than not, as parents, we need to be more mindful of both what we say and how we say it.

Love,
Momma D

My son, if you accept my words and store up my commands within you, turning your ear to wisdom and applying your heart to understanding, indeed, if you call out for insight and cry aloud for understanding, and if you look for it as for silver and search for it as for hidden treasure, then you will understand the fear of the Lord and find the knowledge of God.
~Proverbs 2:1-5 (NIV)

It's BACK!!!!!!!!

When John and I purchased the farm which had previously been in my family for several generations, the only animals residing there were a few mice and a *huge* black snake. Not a big snake, a *HUGE* snake, well over five feet long.

My first meeting with this over-sized reptile took place when the kids and I were looking around one of the outbuildings. I was carrying Olivia, who was barely a year old, but Elizabeth (three) and Zach (six) were walking beside me when we saw the snake go underneath the building we were about to enter.

Zach asked why we let the snake go instead of trying to get it to come out so we could kill it. My first thought was to tell him it was because the snake was big enough to swallow children whole, but don't worry, I didn't say that. Instead, I said something to the effect that the snake wasn't really hurting anything, but that he (Zach) needed to stay away from the building.

Fast forward several weeks. Zach decided he was going to take his tractors and dump truck out to play in the yard. So with his toys in his arms, he opened the door and started to step onto the porch when in a panic he slammed the door shut, dropped his toys, plastered himself against the door, and said, "It's back!"

"It" was the snake—sunning himself on the front stoop (from which he hung over both sides). Apparently, this snake thought his territory extended to the house...*our* house! But did I have news for him.

Telling the kids to stay inside, I went outside via another door, got the hoe, and made sure that snake never found his way to our porch again (or anywhere else, for that matter).

I can still see Zach plastered against the door, eyes as big as dinner plates from the shock of nearly stepping on the snake as he headed out to play. But that's not the only thing I think about when I think about that day.

I think about the fact that, all too often, parents ignore their child's problems, hoping that if they don't acknowledge them, they will stay hidden like a snake underneath a deserted outbuilding. After all, if you don't talk about it or can't see it, it's not there, right? *Wrong!* Just like the snake left the shed to absorb the warmth of the sun, a problem will always surface to the light sooner or later.

If you don't acknowledge the problems in your child's life and help them deal with them appropriately, they will fester and grow and eventually invade your child's life, robbing them of feeling safe, secure, and confident.

I'm not talking about getting involved in spats between friends, or taking on the system because your child didn't make first string on the team, or blaming someone—anyone—for the mistakes your child makes. The problems I'm talking about are genuine difficulties at school, being bullied or even being the bully, physical limitations, difficulties with learning, behavioral problems, emotional anxiety, and self-esteem.

In order for Zach and his little sisters to feel (and actually be) safe when going outside to play, the snake had to go. Likewise, threats to your child's safety, security, and well-being need to be dealt with appropriately so that your child doesn't have to be afraid to step out the front door and live life to the fullest.

Love,
Momma D

In peace I will lie down and sleep, for you alone, Lord, make me dwell in safety. ~Psalm 4:8 (NIV)

T-Shirts Don't Look Good on Me

By the time Elizabeth was three she knew quite a bit—how to write and recognize the letters of the alphabet, the words to countless songs, how to count, her colors, shapes, and opposites. She also knew she didn't look good in a T-shirt.

It was Halloween night, and John took Zach (six), Elizabeth (three), and Olivia (one) to the downtown merchants in our community to go trick-or-treating. Zach was excited when they arrived at the local screen printing shop and discovered they were giving out free T-shirts instead of candy. Elizabeth, on the other hand, smiled politely and said, "No, thank you. T-shirts don't look good on me." John also smiled at the now-dumbfounded hander-out-of-T-shirts and accepted the T-shirt on Elizabeth's behalf.

While most of you probably don't have a child who happily turns down a free T-shirt, you all have a child who, like Elizabeth, has a mind of his/her own. They have definite likes and dislikes and things that interest them versus things that bore them to tears. Your job as their parent is to:

1. Allow your children to express these thoughts and feelings. So Elizabeth didn't like T-shirts. No big deal. I don't like the color blue, and no one has a problem with that.

2. Teach your children to express these thoughts and feelings appropriately. Phrases like "No thank you," "I don't want any, thank you, and" "I'd rather have…" are appropriate. Phrases like "I hate that," "No," and "Yuk" or "Gross" are not.

3. Encourage your children to grow and mature using these thoughts and feelings. Developing a sense of style or personality is not a bad thing. Enjoying books and music instead of soccer or baseball has its merits. Preferring art to math is not the end of the world.

4. Give your children the freedom to embrace and change these thoughts and feelings.

Elizabeth decided to become a nurse before she was ten, and she's a compassionate, gifted nurse, at that. As for the T-shirt thing, she outgrew it a few years later. These days you can find her sporting one just about any day of the week. And she looks just fine.

So remember, the opinionated little person sitting across from you at the dinner table isn't trying to make your life difficult. He or she is just letting you know who they are and what they're all about.

Love,
Momma D

For as in one body we have many members, and the members
do not all have the same function, so we, though many, are one
body in Christ, and individually members one of another.
Having gifts that differ according to the grace given to us, let
us use them: if prophecy, in proportion to our faith; if service,
in our serving; the one who teaches, in his teaching; the one
who exhorts, in his exhortation; the one who contributes, in
generosity; the one who leads, with zeal; the one who does acts
of mercy, with cheerfulness.
~Romans 12:4-8 (NIV)

The Investment with the Highest Return

My granny taught me so many things—how to garden, how to can fruits and vegetables, how to make jellies, wilted lettuce, and cottage cheese, how to churn butter, and the list goes on and on and on. I'm able to do many things most people these days don't even realize *can* be done outside of a factory, all because of Granny. But it's not so much *what* she taught me as *how* she taught me.

Granny was never in too much of a hurry to let me do things with her. From the time I was about five years old, we worked side by side. She patiently showed me what to do and how to do it right. I can't count the times she'd say, "I'll tell you like my mom always told me…if you don't do it right the first time, you'll get the privilege of doing it again."

It would have been so much easier (and quicker) for her to do things herself, but she didn't. She could have used the 'watch me so you'll know what to do when you get older' approach, but she didn't. No, instead, Granny used the hands-on approach to teaching me to be a woman who knew how to provide for her home and her family.

As mothers, grandmothers, aunts, and teachers, we need to take a lesson from Granny. Each time we pass up the opportunity to walk a little slower to allow little feet to keep up with us, or deny ourselves the privilege of sweeping up an extra cup of flour off the floor after baking a batch of cookies, or opt for flower beds with flowers perfectly color coordinated and spaced instead of one with a more whimsical look, we have passed up a golden opportunity to make special memories with the children we love. These moments—I call them *teachable moments*—are lost forever once they pass, so see them for the treasures they are and make the most of them whenever you get the chance.

The memories we have of the special people in our lives are the result of their ability to see these teachable moments for what they are. In other words, these people took the time to invest in us and in our lives. And in turn, we need to make a similar investment into the lives of the young people we love. Think of it as the emotional circle of life.

I couldn't possibly talk this emotional circle of life and investing yourself in someone's life without talking about Carol Bennett. She touched hundreds of lives and invested a part of herself in each and every one of them.

Carol Bennett was my daughter, Elizabeth's, kindergarten teacher. She had been teaching for many years when Elizabeth had her and was nearing the end of her career. But Carol was a good teacher, and it was obvious she truly cared about her students. But never in a million years would I have imagined she would continue to care so many years later.

Fast forward from kindergarten to Elizabeth's senior year in high school. Graduation was approaching, and Elizabeth was receiving gifts and cards from family and friends. One evening as she was opening the mail she had received, I heard her say, "Oh isn't that so sweet!" I was just about to ask her what she thought was so sweet when she sat a card and picture down in my lap. The card was from her kindergarten teacher, Mrs. Bennett. It read, "I'm proud to have been a part of your education. Good luck in the future." The picture was one Elizabeth had drawn in kindergarten!

Each year, Carol Bennett kept one picture from each of her students. And thirteen years later, she took the time to send it—along with a card of congratulations—to each student who was still in the area. Carol had retired two or three years after Elizabeth had been in her class, so the fact that she wasn't even involved in the school system anymore and had a plethora of other things she could have been doing with her time made it even more special. I know I don't need to tell you this, but Carol Bennett is someone who cares!

Remember…at the heart of some of our most treasured memories is the fact that someone like Granny or Carol let us know how much we meant to them. Whose memories are you helping to make?

Love,
Momma D

Likewise, teach the older women to be reverent in the way they
live, not to be slanderers or addicted to much wine, but to teach
what is good. Then they can urge the younger women to love
their husbands and children, to be self-controlled and pure, to
be busy at home, to be kind, and to be subject to their husbands,
so that no one will malign the word of God.
~Titus 2:3-5 (NIV)

We Didn't Have Cable TV and My Kids Have Never Been to Disneyland...Should I Be Worried?

John and I raised our kids in house that was less than 2,000 square feet in size. All three girls shared a bedroom for several years, no one had their own bathroom (not even John and me), we didn't have cable television until Emma was fourteen and the only one left at home, family vacations consisted of camping trips and county fairs for showing livestock, and our kids actually had chores they were expected to do and do correctly. And guess what...they all lived to tell about it!

Don't get me wrong—when one of their friends asked why they lived in such a little house or told them they were sorry they didn't have cable, my heart would skip a beat in fear it would embarrass my kids. Or when they talked about how so-and-so was going to Disney World or on a cruise over spring break, I can't deny I sometimes wished we could do something like that for them.

I'm thankful and proud, however, that none of that seemed to bother our children. They had fields and outbuildings to play in, bikes to ride, pets to play with, a swimming pool to cool off in, a swing set and tree swing to enjoy, and toys which allowed them to be creative and imaginative. They were loved, well-fed, stuck with me all day (they were my career), and provided a life that was about a lot more than stuff.

What's the point, you ask? The point is this: Your children don't need half the things you think they do. They don't need video games and television to stimulate their minds. They need an empty box and an old blanket to do that. They don't need expensive vacations to make family memories. They need board games and popcorn, fishing and camping trips, or games of hide-n-seek and lightening bugs in jars to do that. And finally, they don't need big houses because houses don't make homes—people do.

So the answer to my question *Should I be worried?* is NO! And you shouldn't be, either.

I can say this with complete confidence because Zach, Elizabeth, Olivia, and Emma will readily admit to having great memories of growing up in a little house on a farm , taking family camping trips, and watching *Darkwing Duck* and reruns of 7th *Heaven* instead of whatever the newest shows were at the time. Not only that, all four are happy, loving, and intelligent. They are loving and supportive spouses and parents and have good people skills. What's more, they did it all without a ride down Space Mountain or having fifty-two channels to choose from. However did that happen?

Love,

Momma D

Therefore I tell you, do not worry about your life, what you will eat or drink; or about your body, what you will wear. Is not life more than food, and the body more than clothes? Look at the birds of the air; they do not sow or reap or store away in barns, and yet your heavenly Father feeds them. Are you not much more valuable than they? Can any one of you by worrying add a single hour to your life? And why do you worry about clothes? See how the flowers of the field grow. They do not labor or spin. Yet I tell you that not even Solomon in all his splendor was dressed like one of these. If that is how God clothes the grass of the field, which is here today and tomorrow is thrown into the fire, will he not much more clothe you—you of little faith? So do not worry, saying, 'What shall we eat?' or 'What shall we drink?' or 'What shall we wear?' For the pagans run after all these things, and your heavenly Father knows that you need them. But seek first his kingdom and his righteousness, and all these things will be given to you as well.
~*Matthew 6:25-33 (NIV)*

And Then Erin Came Back

One summer day, I said good-bye to several teenagers I've watched grow up—wishing them the best as they got ready to leave for college, encouraging them to remain true to their faith and relationship with God, and promising to stay in touch. As I was doing so, though, a mental picture of my daughter Emma and her pet turtle, Erin, flashed into my mind.

I don't remember the exact circumstances of how we found Erin. What I do remember, though, is how much Emma loved her tiny little pet. And with a shell diameter of not more than three inches, she (we assumed it was a she) was the smallest turtle I'd ever seen other than the ones they sold in pet stores years ago.

Erin's box house immediately took up residence next to Emma's bed. She was fed vegetables, her water was kept fresh, and said house was kept clean and odor-free. In other words, Emma's skills as a turtle's mom were first-rate. But a little more than a year later, Emma's love for Erin took a right turn down the road of unselfishness when she made the choice to do what was best for Erin. Emma announced it was time to let Erin go back to her natural environment. She wasn't bored with taking care of her turtle or wanting to rid herself of the responsibility. No, with all the wisdom a little girl of seven or eight could have, she just knew it was time for Erin to live life as a turtle was meant to.

So with the help of Elizabeth and Olivia, Emma (with tears streaming down her face) carried Erin to the edge of the woods, said her good-byes, and watched Erin take off for the great unknown. She only watched for a minute or two, however, before running back to the house crying.

When a fair amount of time had passed, and Emma was still crying and wishing she had Erin back, Elizabeth and Olivia told me they were going to go find Erin. Yah, right, I thought. Like that is going to happen. But I didn't say that. I just told them to be careful and not get their hopes up because Erin was most likely a lot farther away than they were allowed to go. Wrong! The girls weren't gone any time before they came running back in…carrying Erin! It turns out Erin wasn't so crazy about being all alone in the world. That silly turtle was actually in the yard heading toward the house! I don't need to tell you what happened next.

One of the most bittersweet moments of being a parent is the moment in which your child leaves home for the last time as a kid on their way to becoming an adult. We are happy, excited, thankful, proud, worried, sad, melancholy, and possibly even relieved (hey, honesty is the best policy). We want them to be productive, happy, and self-sufficient—that's what we raise them to be. But take it from me—that still won't make those tugs on your heartstrings hurt any less.

So what's a parent to do? Let them go and wait for them to come back on their own. When you parent from the heart— loving, nurturing, and teaching your children to be their best possible self—they will leave. They need to leave. But the same things that gave them the power and desire to leave will bring them back again better than ever!

Love,
Momma D

I prayed for this child, and the Lord has granted me what I asked of him. So now I give him to the Lord. For his whole life he will be given over to the Lord." And he worshiped the Lord there.
~1st Samuel 1:27-28 (NIV)

Bubba, Thanks for Asking

With four children, you can be sure things could get pretty loud and chaotic in our house at times. Believe me, I've heard my share of "he did..." and "she did it first..." and "she took my..." and "tell him to stop" and...well, you get the picture.

But there were plenty of good times, too—times when it was obvious they would rather be together than anywhere else and times when their love for one another was bigger and louder than any argument they ever had. Thankfully the good times were more plentiful than the not-so-good ones, but one such moment I know I will never forget happened one night when Zach took Emma on a "date."

We had spent most of the week showing livestock at the fair. The fair ended on Saturday night. We had taken the animals home and had gotten everything put away when Zach, who was sixteen, asked if he could go back to the demolition derby and if he could take four-year-old Emma with him. We agreed but said they couldn't stay too late. And off they went.

They came home a little after ten. Emma was obviously sleepy and immediately started toward her bedroom. But then she stopped, turned around, came back to Zach, and said, "Bubba, thanks for asking me to go with you tonight." And without a moment's hesitation, Zach said, "You're welcome, Emma, and thanks for going with me."

My heart just melted. They *really* did love each other. They still do.

If you have more than one child, there are times when everyone in your house isn't getting along. That's just the way it is. Siblings argue. They fight (sometimes physically). Again...that's just the way it is. *But*...we need to teach our children to love one another and watch out for one another. We have the responsibility to teach our children that siblings are their forever-friends, and that no one will ever be able to fill that spot in their heart.

Love,
Momma D

A friend loves at all times, and a brother is born
for a time of adversity.
~Proverbs 17:17 (NIV)

The Ugly House

One of the high school home ec classes my kids took was called International Foods. It's pretty much just what it sounds like. And it's lots of fun. So much fun, in fact, that the first-semester final is comprised of one task...to construct a gingerbread house complete with cut-out doors and windows and whatever edible decorations the student wishes to use. Sounds like tons of fun, right? That's not what my youngest daughter, Emma would say.

Emma is articulate, knows every muscle and bone in the body, and writes beautiful poetry. She's a wonderful military wife and soon-to-be momma. But she is not a gingerbread house maker. Even the teacher (who has known Emma since the day she was born) had to admit it just wasn't her thing.

Emma didn't even want to bring the thing home. But school policy (I think it was at the janitors' insistence) stated students could not dispose of them at school. So when I picked her up at school the day she was to bring it home, Emma walked out of the school carrying a trash bag holding her gingerbread creation.

My four-year-old granddaughter, Mackenzie, and I both asked to see it. "No," Emma said. "It's really bad. *Really* bad. It's going in the trash dumpster as soon as we get home," Emma insisted.

Mackenzie didn't understand the problem, so persisted in wanting to see what was in the bag until Aunt Emma finally relented. When we got home, we all headed for the trash dumpster to view what Emma considered to be a train wreck of a project. When she lifted the bag off the house, all I could say was, "Emma, you're right. That's bad. *Really* bad. Just toss it." And then we both started laughing so hard we got tears in our eyes.

Now before you pronounce me the world's worst mom, you need to hear me out...

If I would have proclaimed the house to be a work of art, I would have been lying, and she would have known it. I would have been giving her a false sense of self-esteem.

If I would have told Emma she deserved a better grade than what she got, I would have been lying, and she would have known it. I would have been sending her the message that she was being treated unfairly when she wasn't. I would have been giving her a false sense of accomplishment.

Parents, we aren't doing our kids any favors when we tell them they are good at something they clearly aren't. And let's face it...no one is good at everything. So instead of lying to your kids and encouraging them to go after something that makes them feel bad about themselves and doesn't give them a sense of satisfaction, help them find those things they *do* excel and shine in, and then encourage them with everything you've got.

Don't be afraid to tell them their gingerbread house is ugly...as long as you show them each and every day how beautiful you know they are on the inside and help them to know the same.

Love,
Momma D

...keep your tongue from evil and your lips from telling lies.
~Psalm 34:13 (NIV)

The Not-So-Big Mistake

Elizabeth has always been my orderly, methodical one—just like her dad. It has served her well and is just one of the many things about her that makes her the wonderful nurse she is. But once upon a time, Elizabeth had to put aside her design for what she thought the order of things should be.

Elizabeth was more than ready to start kindergarten—so much so that she was only four when she climbed onto that school bus to enter the world of education. She was bright, articulate, and loved to learn. Thankfully, we still had half-day kindergarten because her younger sister and I were more than ready to have her return home to eat lunch with us and tell us all about her first day of school.

She stepped off the bus and immediately started telling me the names of her new friends, how her brother had walked her to her class, and that they had a snack—but she didn't drink her milk (no surprise there). All seemed right in her world. But when we sat down to eat lunch, she looked at me with all the seriousness in the world and said, "Mom, I think I made a big mistake."

"Really? What mistake do you think you made, sweetie?" I asked.

"I think going to school is a mistake," Elizabeth said sadly.

My heart sank. This was something that couldn't be changed. Did I not know my daughter as well as I thought I did? I knew I had to fix this quickly, so I hesitated for only a second before I asked Elizabeth why she thought going to school was a mistake.

"Mom," she said with a mix of sadness and disappointment, "They didn't teach me to read."

Talk about relief! I almost laughed out loud I was so relieved. But I didn't. This was serious stuff to Elizabeth, so it was serious stuff to me, too.

As parents, we sometimes have a been-there-done-that kind of attitude. We know that many of the things our children worry about (like not learning to read on the very first day of kindergarten) aren't nearly as bad as all that. But they don't. And to make them feel small or to insinuate their feelings are unimportant or insignificant is *not* a good thing. Instead of dismissing their feelings as silly or unnecessary, take the time to explain why they don't need to worry and/or how they can (with your help and encouragement) overcome and work through their feelings and concerns.

In Elizabeth's case, it took little more than an explanation of how school works and the assurance that she would learn to read when everyone in the class was ready to learn. Well, that and the promise to start teaching her a few more sight words at home.

The world is a great big and somewhat scary place to children. They need to know that their own little piece of it (aka, home) is safe, nurturing, encouraging, and a place where they will never be made to feel insignificant and will always be listened to.

Love,
Momma D

Anxiety weighs down the heart, but a kind word cheers it up.
~Proverbs 12:25 (NIV)

I Just Love You SO Much

Have you ever been at a loss for words? You knew you should say *something*, but you weren't sure of what that something should be? Of maybe you've done just the opposite. You know, the old open-mouth-insert-foot routine? So what do you do in situations like these?

You might remember your grandma or mom telling you as a child that if you can't say anything nice, don't say anything at all. Sound familiar? Now while I agree with the concept of teaching our children to not say things that are hurtful and unkind, I think we need to take it a step further. I think as parents we need to learn a lesson from my sweet, nearly three-year-old granddaughter, Macy Scout.

Macy loves to talk on the phone. But let's face it—at two and a half, there isn't a whole lot for her to talk about. The dogs, the sheep and cows, what she and her sister have been doing, whether or not she's been in time-out that day, where Grandpa is (and wanting to talk to him)… You know, the normal stuff. But that's usually not enough for Macy—she wants more air time. So what does she do? When she cannot think of anything else to say, she simply says, "I just lub you so, so much, Nanna."

I instantly respond with the same and then she says it again…"I just lub you so, so much, Nanna."

Doesn't that just melt your heart? It sure does mine! The point I want to make, though, is this…

Instead of teaching our children to be silent rather than not say things that are rude or unkind, teach them to **fill that silence** with words that **encourage, mend relationships, melt hearts, and share God's love.** If we teach our children to go that extra step and fill the silence with friendship and love, there won't be near as much room for bullying, gossip, and all those other hurtful things.

Love,
Momma D

Do not let any unwholesome talk come out of your mouths, but only what is helpful for building others up according to their needs, that it may benefit those who listen.
~Ephesians 4:29 (NIV)

Children Should Be Seen and Heard

In the past, children were not encouraged or even allowed to interject themselves into conversations between adults. It was expected that children would sit at the meal table in silence, eating everything on their plates (or being reminded of all the starving orphans). Children weren't expected to speak without being given permission, and they wouldn't dream of interrupting a conversation between adults.

Now while I'm not arguing against children having great manners or against teaching children to have respect for their elders and those in authority, I *am* saying we shouldn't be so quick to dismiss our children. I'm saying we owe it to our children to make them feel validated, to let them know that their thoughts and opinions matter. As a mother of four, I have lived this countless times, but one of the best examples I've experienced that gets to the heart of what I'm saying didn't even come from me.

Raising our children in a small town had its ups and downs…good points as well as not-so-good ones. But one definite advantage was the fact that our church family was small and close-knit. Our four children were loved, talked to, and listened to by everyone—including our preacher, Dave.

Sunday night church service consisted of a small gathering of members from our congregation to study a book of the Bible. This particular Sunday night was to be the first in a series on the book of James. Dave began the study by giving a brief introduction to the book. He started off by saying, "The book of James was written by James, the brother of Jesus." Before he could say one more word, our three-year-old daughter, Emma, who had been lying in the pew, playing with her toys, sat straight up, looked right at Dave, and said, "Well, Dave, I didn't know Jesus had a brother."

Dave, not missing a beat, said, "Well, Emma, he did. In fact, he had four brothers and some sisters, too." Dave then picked up where he left off as if nothing out of the ordinary had taken place. And Emma, who was satisfied with the answer given her, returned to playing (and obviously listening) quietly.

Some of you might be thinking things like "I'd be so embarrassed" or "I would have made sure she knew not to ever do *that* again." Not me and not anyone in the church building that night thought like that. No, to everyone there, Emma was simply a little girl who had a question that deserved an answer. She was not made to feel as if she had said or done anything wrong. She was not scowled at or thought to be rude or naughty. In fact, nearly everyone took the time to compliment her on being a good listener and wanting to know more.

My point is this—children are eager to please us and eager to learn from us. So why, as a parent, would you want to do anything to squelch that? Why would you want to ever give your child the impression that their thoughts and words did not matter or were not wanted? Oh, I know there are times the sheer number of words that come from a preschooler each day are immeasurable, and you feel your ears simply can't take much more. But trust me, all too soon, those years are gone—replaced by teenagers and young adults who won't be nearly as eager to talk to you...*unless* they've had plenty of practice and a captive and eager audience prior to reaching that stage in life.

So my challenge to you is this: Take the time each day to talk to, listen to, and enjoy conversing with your children.

Love,
Momma D

*Don't let anyone look down on you because you are young, but
set an example for the believers in speech, in conduct, in love,
in faith and in purity.
~1ˢᵗ Timothy 4:12 (NIV)*

A Little Work Never Hurt Anyone...Including Kids

My son, Zach, sent me a text message and a picture the other day that brought back a flood of memories. The text told me he had discovered one of his cows had calved, but that the calf had slid under the fence and was covered in snow. And so the challenges of raising a bottle calf began for Zach and Becca. But if you were to ask my granddaughters, Mackenzie and Macy, they would say the *joys* of raising a bottle calf had come their way. I say this because the picture Zach sent with his message was a picture of Mackenzie and Macy with their new responsibility, both girls smiling from ear to ear.

Oh, the memories! Raising our four children on a farm gave them plenty of opportunities to enjoy responsibilities like Mackenzie and Macy have with the new calf. And I can honestly say they were always ready to take turns feeding the bottle calves we raised and the occasional lamb who needed a surrogate mom...or three or four.

Our children willingly (most of the time) did their daily chores, helped in the hay field, and took their turns doing late-night lamb checks during lambing season. There was even that time I needed help tracking down a few goats along a major highway (thanks, Olivia). And through it all, we worked as a family. Don't get me wrong—they weren't perfect. There were times they didn't do what they were expected to do (especially when it came to pulling weeds). But they never resented the fact that they were expected to work. In fact, it gave them a sense of pride. They were proud they were able to do things other kids didn't know how to do. They were proud of the fact that they earned the money to buy their first car or truck and pay for their insurance, cell phone, and the little extras they wanted that didn't fit into our budget.

The lesson I want to leave you with in sharing my memories is that of **responsibility**. Children need responsibility. They should be expected to do regular chores and to help out around the house with the bigger jobs—jobs like cleaning out the garage, getting ready for a yard sale, and yard work. Oh, and did I mention they need to do this without expecting to be paid for everything they do?

That's right. We didn't give our children a regular allowance. They did their chores because that's what being part of a family is all about—working together for the good of everyone. No, we didn't use our children as cheap child labor. They were never made to do things so that we wouldn't have to do anything. We taught them to be responsible by example—by working *with* them.

While our children didn't have everything they wanted (what child should?), they always had everything they needed, and we supported them in their extracurricular activities by making sure their fees were paid, equipment was purchased, practices were attended, and that we were there to cheer them on. Most importantly, however, they knew they were loved and that because we loved them, we wanted to give them something more important than things. We wanted to give them the ability to make their own way and be people of integrity.

Sadly, there are way too many parents who feel that doing everything for their children instead of teaching them to do for themselves is to show them love. But a little work never hurt anyone...including a child. If you don't believe me, take a look around. You won't have to look very far to find a young person lacking in the area of responsibility and work ethics.

That chore chart is looking pretty good now, isn't it?

Love,
Momma D

All hard work brings a profit, but mere talk leads only to poverty.
~Proverbs 14:23 (NIV)

How NOT to Kill a Cat

How many times have you heard someone say something to the effect that kids today are smarter than they used to be? You'll usually hear this in reference to matters of technology, pop culture, and society in general. It's true. Today's children *are* more in tune with what is going on around them, but *knowing* what is happening does *not* mean they *understand* what is happening. No matter how smart you think your children are, they are still children and have a childlike perspective on things (as they should have).

Years ago, John and I, along with Zach, Elizabeth, and Olivia, lived with my granny for about two months while our house was being made ready to live in. But we did not come without a few other family members—including our barn cat and her kittens. Well...one evening Granny fixed chicken and dumplings for supper. She took a bit of the broth containing small bits of chicken in it and gave it to the cats to enjoy with their supper—something she'd done countless times over the years. But as luck would have it, there was a bit of gristle in it, and one of the kittens choked on it and died. But wait, it gets better.

The kitten just happened to be three-year-old Elizabeth's favorite. Being raised on a farm, none of my children were immune to the fact that things die, but when we explained that the kitten had choked on its supper and died, she asked what it had eaten. Granny, who felt bad enough already, was deeply apologetic when she revealed that it was the chicken she had given them for supper (which Elizabeth thought was so sweet of Granny at the time).

Elizabeth shed a few tears and talked about the kitten off and on throughout the next day but after that seemed to be fine. On Sunday, however, Elizabeth's Sunday school teacher could hardly contain her laughter when she told Granny, John, and I what Elizabeth had said in class earlier. When she asked the children what they wanted to pray about, Elizabeth said she wanted prayers for her kitten. The teacher asked what was wrong with the kitten, and Elizabeth matter-of-factly said, "Granny killed my cat."

Today's children *are* exposed to so much more than I was as a child, and that's saying quite a bit since my childhood was spent in the midst of the Kennedy assassinations, the Viet Nam war, the Civil Rights movement, and the era of free love and the hippy culture. But exposure to grown-up matters doesn't guarantee a grown-up perspective of things. As parents, it is essential that you:

1. Do not overload your children with adult information. Let them be children for as long as possible. They have plenty of time to deal with life when they grow up.

2. Ask your children what they think and how they feel about the situations to which they are unavoidably exposed. Knowing their perspective on things will help you help them.

Children are not the mini-adults we sometimes try to make them be. I know as a parent I have been guilty of doing this at times. It's easy to do, but it's just as easy to let them stay little for a little while longer.

Love,
Momma D

And Jesus grew in wisdom and stature, and in favor with God and man.
~Luke 2:52 (NIV)

Miss Congeniality

How many times did your mother tell you that inner beauty is more important than what you look like on the outside? Okay, so maybe it wasn't a coincidence that she said it every time your hair frizzed or you had a pimple in the middle of your forehead...on school picture day. Now I'll ask you how many times you've said the same thing to *your* children?

There's a reason we say that, you know. We say it because it's true. The Bible in 1st Peter 3:3-4 says that "Your beauty should not come from outward adornment, such as elaborate hairstyles and the wearing of gold jewelry or fine clothes. Rather, it should be that of your inner self, the unfading beauty of a gentle and quiet spirit, which is of great worth in God's sight."

As parents, we do our best to impart these pearls of wisdom to our children, but sometimes we wonder how well we are getting the message across. I know I have, but there have also been plenty of times when my heart was happy, happy, happy knowing the message had been received loud and clear.

Being a farm family, one of the highlights of our year came each August—the county fair. The kids looked forward to watching fair-goers come through to view their sheep and cows and to competing with their 4-H friends for ribbons and prize money. But one year, fourteen-year-old Olivia decided to participate in an additional competition...the one for Fair Princess.

I have to admit I was surprised when she announced she wanted to participate in the pageant. Not because I didn't think she was "pageant-worthy," but because Olivia wasn't what you would consider a girly-girl. But since we were going to be there anyway, and it wasn't like she was going against the moms or girls on *Toddlers and Tiaras*, John and I told her to go for it.

It was obvious she was having a good time and was keeping things in the right perspective. I say obvious because whenever I picked her up from pageant practice, she was always talking and laughing with the other girls. She didn't view them as competition. She viewed them as friends.

On the night of the pageant when it was time to announce the winners and runners-up, we couldn't have been happier or prouder when the pageant director explained that the title of Miss Congeniality was voted on by the contestants themselves, and that the winner, Olivia Noble, had received the vote of every one of her fellow contestants.

Olivia was a beautiful girl who has grown into a beautiful young woman. But the brightness in her eyes and her smile aren't just pretty. They are a reflection of the beauty inside her heart and soul.

As parents, you need to be on guard against the world's perception of beauty and protect your children (especially girls) from being caught up in the lies and deceptions that what they look like on the outside is what makes them beautiful, lovable, and valuable. Affirm the characteristics that make them truly beautiful—compassion, kindness, respect, sincerity, honesty, integrity... And proclaim them to be the Miss Congeniality(ies) of your life each and every day.

Love,
Momma D

So God created mankind in his own image, in the image of God
he created them;
male and female he created them.
~Genesis 1:27 (NIV)

Which One Are You?

I recently completed ghostwriting a book on the dangers of being a toxic parent, meaning a parent whose actions and attitudes bring as much or more harm than good to their child. The book was written from a practical and technical point of view—not my usual style, but hey, that's what they wanted, so that's what I wrote. But in doing so, I really started thinking about the fact that there's a world of difference between being a parent and being a mom or dad.

Parenting is defined as the "process of promoting and supporting the physical, emotional, social, and intellectual development of a child from infancy to adulthood." Nothing warm and fuzzy about that, is there? And did you notice there was no mention or even insinuation of love or of being nurturing and sacrificial? How sad is that—for everyone involved!

But like I said, it made me ask myself which one I was when my children were growing up. Was I a parent, or was I a mom?

A parent supplies their children with food, clothes, and a place to live. A parent makes sure their child has the necessary school supplies. A parent drops their child off at church. A parent buys what they think their child will like for Christmas…in September, and then sighs with relief that the job is done. A parent asks "how was it" because they don't take the time to go to their child's games, programs, or other events. A parent makes sure their child receives the medical care they need. A parent allows the obligatory dog or cat, but that's it! A parent's involvement in their child's school is usually nothing more than dutifully attending parent/teacher conferences (maybe). A parent says things like:

- Let me do it, so it will be right.
- I'll do it myself so I can get done quicker.
- Getting a C in math isn't acceptable.

A parent feels they deserve their child's gratitude for "all I do for you." A parent loves their child but often makes direct or implied stipulations or conditions on that love. A parent misses out on the very best reasons for having children.

A mom or dad bakes cookies with their children and doesn't mind the peanut butter being smeared down the handle of the knife and packs their child's lunch for school because they don't like school food. A mom or dad feels their heart will break when they can't afford the shoes or jeans the rest of the kids are wearing and hopes no one makes fun of them and that someday they will understand. A mom or dad's efforts go into making a house a home instead of being concerned about the square footage or the address. A mom or dad does without so their children can have new backpacks, Hello Kitty folders, and money for sports fees. A mom or dad worships with their child, living the religious and moral beliefs they want their child to have. A mom or dad exchanges a doll three times in a month so Santa will leave the right one under the tree and hopes with all their heart that the gifts they give will put a smile on the face and heart of their child. A mom or dad rarely has to ask "how was it" because they were there to greet their child at the finish line or broke their lawn chair bouncing up and down with excitement at the game. A mom or dad goes without sleep for days on end to see their child through an illness. A mom or dad digs out empty jars to house tadpoles and lightening bugs and doesn't mind that sometimes the house feels more like the zoo for wayward mice, frogs, and salamanders. A mom or dad attends school events, volunteers at their child's school, and checks to see if homework is done. A mom or dad says things like:

- Help me do this, so you'll know how.
- You dust the chairs while I do the picture frames.
- I know math is hard for you, but as long as you do your best, that's all that matters.

A mom or dad sees their children as blessings and gifts from God. A mom or dad loves unconditionally with that *just-because* kind of love even if it's not easy or not returned. A mom or dad feels unspeakable joy and pain in raising their children and wouldn't have it any other way.

I'd like to believe I was (and still am) a mom and not just a parent. What about you?

Love,
Momma D

But the fruit of the Spirit is love, joy, peace, forbearance,
kindness, goodness, faithfulness, gentleness and self-control.
Against such things there is no law.
~Galatians 5:22-23 (NIV)

The Story of Hoppy

When you live on a farm, animals are naturally a big part of your life—both in and out of the barn. What's more, with four children, you can be sure the number of animals (aka pets) is going to be a big one. Hoppy was counted in our big number.

One afternoon, Elizabeth and Olivia went to the pond to collect tadpoles in a bucket, but when I saw them coming toward the house, their excitement level was a lot higher than what tadpoles called for. I was right.

Inside the bucket was a bullfrog—a *really big* bullfrog. I'm talking several pounds big. Olivia was ecstatic. She'd caught him with her own two little hands and couldn't wait to set up a little home for him...in her room. Yep, that's right—Hoppy the huge bullfrog was coming inside.

After giving strict instructions as to what would and wouldn't be allowed, I went on about my business and left the girls to creating their frog oasis. Somehow, though, during the transfer from the bucket to said oasis, Hoppy hopped right out of Olivia's hands. Olivia didn't know whether to laugh or cry. All she could do was watch while *I* hopped after Hoppy. And let me tell you, that frog could jump!

Once he was safely secured, I made the executive decision that Hoppy would be living outside on the patio. No argument was made. For the next couple of days, Olivia carefully tended to her new pet. But it didn't take her long to realize that Hoppy wasn't very hoppy anymore...or happy. So being the wise little animal lover she was, she returned Hoppy to his real home from where we heard him often.

Some of you might think I was crazy for ever letting Hoppy into our lives (much less our home). But before you pronounce sentence, think about this: In letting Olivia have her "Hoppy adventure," I allowed her and her siblings to learn some important lessons. They learned:

- That not all animals are destined to be pets.
- That loving something or someone means you do what's best for them instead of making your own selfish desires the focal point of it all.
- That a nurturing, safe, and healthy environment is essential for happiness.
- That bullfrogs can jump higher than they (the kids) were tall.

Love,
Momma D

So do not throw away your confidence; it will be richly rewarded. You need to persevere so that when you have done the will of God, you will receive what he has promised.
~Hebrews 10:35-36 (NIV)

Granny's New Blanket

When you have children in the house, you can be sure there will be accidents—spills, breaks, stains, and any number of other "methods" of turning something new or special into something new or special with a little added character. That's life, and there's not really anything you can do to stop it. But what you *can* do is let your children know that you understand accidents are just that—accidents—and that nothing you own is more important than they are.

Extending this kind of grace is comforting and reassuring to a child. I know this is true because my granny was the best at it.

One Friday evening when I was five, Granny came home from the grocery store with three things I thought were the best treats anyone could ask for: potato chips, French onion dip, and a new orange wool blanket with satin edging around it. Wow!

The chips and dip were great, but that blanket... All we had were handmade quilts, and I thought that blanket was the prettiest thing I'd ever seen. NOTE: Thankfully I'm a lot smarter now and appreciate the beauty of those quilts.

Later on in the evening, I had a bowl of chips and dip and was then tucked into bed with that glorious orange blanket wrapped around me. A few hours later, however, I woke up not feeling very well. Too much of a good thing, I guess. I won't go into details, but let's just say the orange blanket wasn't very pretty anymore. I was heartbroken. I'd ruined Granny's brand-new blanket. I remember crying and repeatedly telling her how sorry I was. But in true Granny-fashion, she just cleaned me up and said, "There's nothing to be sorry about. It's just a blanket. It will wash. So don't cry, just come sit with me so I can make sure *you* are alright." Then she gave me a kiss and held me on her lap for a while before tucking me back into a clean bed for the rest of the night.

Now I know that may not seem like much to some people, but to five-year-old me, that was the ultimate display of love, for Granny to care more about me than she did about a brand-new blanket.

Forty-seven years later, I still have that orange blanket. When Granny died almost two years ago, it was one of the few things I needed to keep as I prepared to sell her things. The satin edging is long gone, and it's been washed more times than I can count. But looking at that blanket reminds me that it is both an honor and responsibility to extend to our children the same grace God gives us and to let them know they are more valuable than all the blankets (or anything else) in the world.

How about your children? Do your children know they are your greatest treasure? Does your love reflect an attitude that says things can be washed, mended, or replaced...but they can't?

Love,
Momma D

Then he said to them, "Watch out! Be on your guard against all kinds of greed; life does not consist in an abundance of possessions."
~Luke 12:15 (NIV)

Do We Have To??

As a law enforcement officer, John worked all different shifts—days, evenings, and nights. There were both advantages and disadvantages to the different hours, but one disadvantage was that he sometimes had to miss the kids' evening activities. While it usually wasn't a problem for me to take them, one evening in June of 1995, it was particularly chaotic and stressful. It was the evening of our monthly 4-H meeting, and our family was responsible for snacks for the evening. Emma was a couple of months old and had gotten her first shots earlier in the afternoon, and we'd had to stop at Wal-Mart to get drinks to go with the snacks we were taking to 4-H.

Because we were running so short on time, we ate supper at the McDonald's inside the store. I still remember telling my three children to hurry up and eat so we wouldn't be late. And I still remember feeling bad about rushing them. It wasn't all that often that we ate out (yes, eating at the Wal-Mart McDonald's was eating out back then), so they were enjoying this special treat. After the third or fourth "quit talking and eat," twelve-year-old Zach asked with all the sincerity in the world, "Why do we have to go?" Well, it's 4-H and you're in the club and… "Do we have to be in 4-H?" he asked.

Are you kidding, I thought? They loved 4-H...or at least I thought they did. "Don't you want to be in 4-H anymore," I asked. A resounding no was the reply. They liked the other kids, and they liked what they did, but they *didn't* like being rushed and hurried. They were tired. Zach and Elizabeth rationalized that not being in 4-H wouldn't make them any less of a farmer. Who would have thought they'd be thinking more clearly than I was? I plead excess tiredness due to just having had baby number four. But they were making perfect sense. So right then and there we decided they would quit 4-H until they decided they wanted to rejoin (*if* they decided to rejoin). I explained that it would be rude to default on our responsibility to take the snacks that evening, however, so after smiles, sighs of relief, and allowing the kids to finish without shoving their food down their throats, we went to our last meeting for many, many years.

To all you parents out there who are tempted to sign your children up for every possible sport and extracurricular activity, I say *don't*! Don't think you need to fill every hour of every day of their lives. You don't. Children need a good amount of time to just *be* and to play like a kid (because that is what they are). Don't try to live vicariously through your children, using the excuse that you want them to have the things you never did. Instead, let them be their own unique selves. Don't press them to become skilled and devoted to a sport or activity in an attempt to put them at the head of the line and on the road to college scholarships. That's placing far too much pressure on a child, and it's just not good parenting no matter how you try to justify it.

Children are going to get excited (initially) about anything that looks fun, and they are going to ask you to sign them up. Don't cave. They don't know what they are asking for. Instead, be the parent...the sensible kind of parent who limits their child to church and one additional activity. Trust me, that's all a child needs to be allowed to participate in. If you don't believe me, ask yourself this...when is the last time you had time to be silly with your kids, snuggle with your kids, or just be with your kids without saying we've got to hurry or we'll be late for...?

Love,
Momma D

A little sleep, a little slumber,
a little folding of the hands to rest.
~Proverbs 6:10 (NIV)

A Valentine for Marge

As parents, we try to raise our children to be kind and honest and to respect themselves and others. One way John and I did this was by giving our children the gift of old people.

Now before you start thinking I'm being insensitive or disrespectful, let me explain. We were always conscious of making sure our children knew the older people in their lives—not just by looking at them from across the room or grinning and bearing a few cheek-pinching extended family members, but really knowing them and counting them as friends.

Over the years, I've been blessed to receive a number of affirmations from each of my children that we'd been successful in this endeavor, but one particular incident is especially dear to my heart.

Emma was three years old and excited to be scribbling her name on the back of her Little Mermaid valentine cards just like her siblings were. On the Saturday before Valentine's Day that year, they were filling out cards to take to their friends at church the following day. Emma was telling me who she wanted to make cards for, and at the top of her list was Marge. Marge was a sweet little lady who was in her eighties. She barely spoke above a whisper and was really a bit on the shy side, but she loved Emma, and Emma wanted to make sure Marge knew the feeling was mutual by giving her the brightest, most sparkling card in the box.

I can still see Emma running to Marge to hand her the card and the hugs and smiles that followed after she opened it. Emma had the gift of having Marge in her life.

Giving your children the gift of old people in their lives should be among your top priorities. In doing so, your children are exposed to the wisdom of those who've lived longer. They enjoy the fact that older people often have time and patience to be with children. Children are seen as a welcome breath of fresh air and energy by many old people. Your children learn endurance, integrity, and the value of commitment and responsibility from the older people in their lives, as well as a number of other character traits we should possess. And it all happens just because two separate and very different generations walk the common ground called friendship.

I know they can learn these things from you, too. And they should. But there's just something about different generations spending time together—forming an actual relationship—that plants these life lessons deeper within our hearts and minds.

Love,

Momma D

Stand up in the presence of the aged, show respect for the
elderly and revere your God. I am the Lord.
~Leviticus 19:32 (NIV)

Granny Love

There is nothing a child wants any more in this world than to know they are loved. Not loved because they are cute or because they made a goal the first time they played soccer. Not loved because they get the lead role in the school play or because they memorized the most Bible verses in Sunday school. Not loved because they are going to carry on the family business or because they graduated with honors. Every child longs...needs...deserves to be loved just because.

Most people will call this *unconditional love*. I call it *Granny love*. I call it Granny love because it's the kind of love I grew up with—the kind Granny loved me with from the day I was born until the day she died last October.

When people would comment about the obvious closeness of our relationship, I would often laugh and say, "She couldn't or wouldn't love me any less if I was a serial killer." I'd say it laughingly, but I can't even begin to explain how good it felt...how comforting it was to know it was there.

The last several years of Granny's life left her unable to remember almost everything—everything but who I was and how much we loved one another. It made me sad to deal with the disappearance of her memory and simple life skills, but it was always a blessing and an honor to do so. It made me sad to see the frustration and fear in her eyes, knowing she should remember something but didn't. But it was easy for me to fill in the gaps and keep going. It was easy because it was all done with and because of love.

What hasn't been easy is going on without the Granny love I'd had for so long—fifty-two years, to be exact. I was lying on the bed beside Granny when she took her last breath on my fifty-second birthday last October. I know in my head and in my heart that she is free from all she'd endured over the last several years. I know in my head and heart that I will see her again in Heaven.

But I also know that no matter how old you are, you never really quit being a child when it comes to needing and desiring that just-because kind of love—Granny love.

Knowing that Granny love is gone has left a hole in my heart that no one—not even my husband, kids, or grandkids—can fill. That space was there for only her and me.

While I certainly don't claim to be the perfect mom, my four children will tell you that if they know nothing else, at the end of the day, they know one thing…that Mom loves them Granny-style. They know there is a place in their hearts and mine that is only for me and them. It's a place that will never shrink or go away.

As a parent, you owe it to your children to carve out that Granny love space in their hearts. You owe it to them to give them the peace and comfort of knowing that even if they were a serial killer, you would love them to the moon and back.

Love,
Momma D

Above all, love each other deeply, because love covers over a
multitude of sins.
~1st Peter 4:8 (NIV)

It's a Great Day to Be Alive

Back in the winter of 2000, Travis Tritt released the hit song, "It's a Great Day to be Alive." It goes something like this... "It's a great day to be alive; I know the sun's still shinin' when I close my eyes; There's some hard times in the neighborhood; But why can't every day be just this good..."

You may or may not remember the song, but I know I will never forget it. Here's why...

My daughter, Emma, loves to sing and has always had a knack for picking up the lyrics to every song she hears almost immediately—this song included. Anyway...one day in the summer of 2001, when Emma was five, I instructed her to get out of the swimming pool and dry off while I started fixing dinner. Emma's mode of drying off was usually the swing set, so off she went. She loved to swing just as high as she could, her long hair trailing behind her. But she didn't just swing. She usually sang while she was sailing through the air. And yep, you guessed it...as I worked in the kitchen getting dinner, I was serenaded by Emma singing "It's a Great Day to be Alive" at the top of her lungs. But Emma wasn't just singing the song...she *believed* the song.

I can still hear that little voice and see that Little Mermaid swimming suit flying through the air. It was one of the most profound moments of my life. She believed with her whole being that it really was a great day to be alive. She was safe, happy, loved, secure...everything a child deserves to be.

As parents, our goal should be to make every day a great day for our children to be alive. No, not by giving them everything they think they want and need. No, not by working nonstop to be able to take them on exotic or expensive vacations. No, not by providing them with a house so big you have to look to find one another.

As parents, our goal should be to make every day a day our children know for sure and for certain that they are safe, happy, loved, secure…everything a child deserves to be.

Love,
Momma D

Therefore if you have any encouragement from being united with Christ, if any comfort from his love, if any common sharing in the Spirit, if any tenderness and compassion, then make my joy complete by being like-minded, having the same love, being one in spirit and of one mind. Do nothing out of selfish ambition or vain conceit. Rather, in humility value others above yourselves, not looking to your own interests but each of you to the interests of the others.
~Philippians 2:1-4 (NIV)

The Chronicles of My Heart

As I sat rocking two-day-old Olivia, I was overwhelmed with the need to tell her how thankful I was that the three months of bed rest I'd been on resulted in her coming *only* one month early. I wanted her to know how thankful I was for her perfect and beautiful being and how full of hope I was for the life she had ahead of her. But she wouldn't have understood, so I just held her close, hoping she would feel my love.

Across the room, five-year-old Zach and one-and-a-half-year-old Elizabeth sat playing. I wanted desperately to let Zach know how much I appreciated his willingness to play with his little sister and to share with him my feelings of pride, excitement, and apprehension in regards to his entering kindergarten in the fall. I wanted him to know what a joy it was to watch him help his daddy in every way possible. I wanted to tell Elizabeth how proud (and relieved) I was that she had decided on her own to be a big girl and use the potty all by herself and praise her for knowing her colors and being able to recognize the letters of the alphabet already. I wanted to tell them what a great job they were doing in welcoming their new baby sister to the family. But anything beyond "Good job, honey" or "I'm so proud of you!" would have gone right over their heads. So I just smiled and told them I loved them.

But my heart kept telling me that wasn't enough, so while the girls slept peacefully and Zach was diligently hauling countless loads of dirt and gravel around the yard with his dump truck and tractor, I conveyed my thoughts to them the best way I knew how—I wrote each of them a letter. As I finished the last letter, I decided these letters would be the first of many more to come. I decided that throughout my lifetime, I would periodically write letters to my children, letters that would provide insight as to what it was like to be their mother. I wanted my children to have the chronicles of my heart.

The number of letters I wrote increased to four when Emma was born, but that was fine—I had plenty to write about! Over the last twenty-five years, my letters have disclosed the joys and disappointments (yes, our children do disappoint us at times) their lives have brought into mine, the pride I feel in who they are, and the ache in my heart that matched (or exceeded) the ache in theirs when they were hurting. The letters I have written contain words of encouragement as well as chastisement and have served to preserve memories of the special moments in their lives. The little things they said and did that often fade from our memory when the moment is past are forever recorded for their sake as well as mine.

I sometimes wonder what effect these letters will have on my children. Will my words bring smiles and happy tears to their faces the way they did mine? Will their questions be answered as to why I did the things I did? Will they commiserate with me when they read my words of worry and concern because they are feeling the same in regards to their own children?

There have been times I have contemplated not writing any more letters and letting my children have them, but I know now that isn't going to happen. I'm not finished writing yet. I am still breathing, so I am still their mother. It's not much, but their letters will be a part of their inheritance—a legacy of who they are in their mother's eyes. I want their letters to serve as a window to their childhood—an affirmation of how loved and valued they are just because they get up each morning and take a breath. I want the letters to serve as tools of accountability for them to live their lives as the man/women of God they were raised to be.

Zachery, Elizabeth, Olivia, and Emma wake up each morning in their own homes and live their own lives. But they also wake up knowing they are loved to the fullest. I have never used my letter writing as a substitute for letting my children know how precious they are to me. But these letters—the chronicles of my heart—will be the proof they can hold on to long after I am gone.

So if you don't want to risk letting another memory fade with time or want to explain why you did what you did, but knew it would fall on deaf ears, ears unable (or unwilling) to comprehend, I encourage you to pick up a pen and paper and start writing. It doesn't matter if you write a lifetime's worth of letters, or just a few. What matters is that you leave your children something tangible to cling to when you are gone.

Love,

Momma D

We will not hide them from their descendants; we will tell the next generation the praiseworthy deeds of the Lord, his power, and the wonders he has done.
~Psalm 78:4 (NIV)

About the Author

As an author/writer, **DARLA NOBLE** spend much of her time putting words on paper (both the real and virtual kind) in hopes that people will read them, be encouraged by them, and become better people for having read what she writes.

When she's not writing, she's spending time with her husband of 36 years, their four children, children in-law, and nearly-perfect grandchildren. And when she's not with them, she can be found in her garden, reading a book, or being involved in various church activities.

You can follow her on Twitter and "Like" her on Facebook (dnoblewrites).

Made in the USA
Columbia, SC
06 May 2018